GRANDMA ONLINE

Grandma
ONLINE

A Grandmother's Guide to the Internet

Kathleen Shaputis

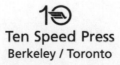

Ten Speed Press
Berkeley / Toronto

A Kirsty Melville Book

1☉

Ten Speed Press
P.O. Box 7123
Berkeley, California 94707
www.tenspeed.com

Distributed in Australia by Simon and Schuster Australia, in Canada by Ten Speed Press Canada, in New Zealand by Southern Publishers Group, in South Africa by Real Books, in Southeast Asia by Berkeley Books, and in the United Kingdom and Europe by Airlift Book Company.

Cover design by Jennifer Barry Design
Interior design by Betsy Stromberg

Library of Congress Cataloging-in-Publication Data

Shaputis, Kathleen.
   Grandma online: a grandmother's guide to the Internet/Kathleen Shaputis.
      p. cm.
   "Kirsty Melville Book"-T.p. verso.
   ISBN 1-58008-255-6
   1. Internet-Handbooks, manuals, etc. 2. Grandmothers-Computer network resources-Handbooks, manuals, etc. 3. World Wide Web-Directories. I. Title.

TK5105.875.I57 S495 2001
025.04-dc21   2001027172

First printing, 2001
Printed in Canada

1 2 3 4 5 6 7 8 9 10 - 05 04 03 02 01

TO MY MOM
(I will always miss you)

TO GRAMMA JEAN
the best fairy grandmother of all

Contents

ACKNOWLEDGMENTS

If it takes a village to raise a child, it takes almost as many people to create a book. I am fortunate to have many wonderful people to thank for their care and support during the evolution of *Grandma Online*. I don't mean to leave anyone out—please know you are all appreciated and cherished. I do, however, want to thank a few people in particular.

First and foremost I need to thank Eva Shaw, Ph.D., my mentor and best-selling author of such terrific books as *How to Write a Non-Fiction Book*, *What to Do When a Loved One Dies*, and more. Eva's enthusiasm and energy, let alone her tremendous talent as a writer and instructor, were the cornerstones of motivation for me over the past few years. If you can get into one of her classes, run—don't walk—to register. Visit her Web site at www.EvaShaw.com.

Next I must bow in gratitude to Jean Butera, who is my daily taskmaster and friend as well as the president of my fan club. Jean is an emotional icon for me and the cherished adopted grandmother of Joshua and Isaiah, my grandsons. Her unlikely e-mail threats to show up, sit up, and keep working balanced her generous accolades throughout the life of this book.

In Rancho Cucamonga, my applause for their continuous cheerleading and creative hearts go to the fabulous Kay Murphy and Lola de Julio de Maci, as well as the rest of the Friday night Barnes & Noble writers' group who were there at the beginning of this roller coaster ride. This includes transplanted Rusty without whom the Web site for *Grandma Online* would have taken twice as long to get up and running.

In Chino, my promotion team consists of the most precious grandmothers anyone could have in their corner: Betty, Tana, Debora, Lenna, Jessie (in her New York state of mind), Carolyn, and Velma as well as my non-grandma members, Doreen, Paula, Shani, Marilyn, Richard, and many, many others. The rest of the Southern California sideline seats hold family with Aunt Fran, Jamie, Colleen, and Sherry Ann leading the yells. I wish I could list everyone who has helped, but my editor told me the acknowledgments couldn't be longer than the book.

In Olympia, I found an esoteric spirit of acceptance in other writers at my own Olympia Writers Group, the members of which were there for me Wednesday nights at the local Barnes & Noble. Their powers of listening, support, and encouragement were invaluable. Special thanks go to Pat Swan.

My sincerest gratitude goes to Dr. Lillian Carson, author of *The Essential Grandparent*, in writing the foreword to this book. Her work and talent are appreciated in assisting a new author on the block.

Most important, I must thank Kirsty Melville, my publisher at Ten Speed Press, for her commitment and support of *Grandma Online*. And additional appreciation goes to Windy Ferges, my editor, for her talent and positive personality throughout the process.

Last, but never least, are the men in my life who have colored this project in their own loving ways: my dad, who has endured my stories with a smile in his heart since I was a little girl; my husband, Bob, who offered me the freedom of no excuses to write and who is still waiting for his boat; and all the grandsons that made me what I am today.

FOREWORD

There isn't a better way to herald the new millennium than by becoming computer savvy. *Grandma Online* challenges all Luddites to lay down their objections and to "get with the program," especially if they happen to be grandmas.

To fulfill our roles as essential grandparents, we must keep up with our grandchildren. They need us, and it's healthy for us to be connected to the young. Our grandchildren thrive on the unconditional love, wisdom, companionship, and care we offer. Our stories build bridges between them and their ancestors. We inform them that they belong to a family with a history and roots. Our belief in them fosters their belief in themselves and encourages them to spread their wings. And believe it or not, being online can help us fulfill these tasks.

Without the advantage of growing up with computers in our homes or classrooms, many grandparents tend to view computers as a hassle to avoid. It is easy to understand that, to the uninitiated, computer technology and lingo are intimidating. And after all, who needs it anyway?

Well, *you* do . . . and Kathleen Shaputis tells you just how to become computer savvy with her thoughtful and humorous step-by-step guidance. No longer will you feel like a computer dummy. She clears up the mysteries surrounding this new technology with practical suggestions for making the choices that will serve you best.

Then comes the real fun. She tantalizes the reader by waving the carrot of being online and whetting our imaginations with the myriad possibilities it offers. You can shop till you drop and find treasures for your grandchildren. Does your grandchild want superhero party decorations that are no longer in the stores? Well, be a grandma hero and find them online.

There are so many creative ideas for grandparents in this book that it will become an invaluable reference book. And don't forget how being online can broaden our own lives with information, keeping us current with the latest news, weather reports, and happenings.

My personal favorite is the use of e-mail. Even if your grandchildren live a short distance away, you can still e-mail them at any time of the day or night without worry that you are interrupting their homework or interfering with dinner or bedtime. Send your message whenever you have the urge. It's a great way to remind them that they have a grandma who is thinking of them.

It's true that learning how to use the computer and connecting to the Internet takes some time, but in the long run, it will simplify your life. So take the plunge, Grandma. Enhance your grandparenting by letting Gramma Kathleen's humor and support guide you into cyberspace.

Dr. Lillian Carson

Who's playing the biological jokes around here? One day I woke up from my busy and intense life in the connector lane of the local freeway to find myself called "Grandmother." I'm not old enough to be a grandmother; why, I'm just . . . I'm just . . . well. Okay, I'll admit I'm physically old enough to be a grandmother. I was there in front of the television set watching the original black-and-white Mouseketeer episodes; I bonded with Annette and Sharon. But hey, emotionally and mentally, when I became a grandmother, I wasn't ready to count myself in that matriarch category yet.

I guess I should take heart that at this fantastic age in my life I'm the grandmother of California-grown Joshua, Isaiah, and Texas Taylor, and not the mom. So many of my generation decided to put off being parents until the last possible moment and are now changing dirty diapers while watching the balance amounts on their IRAs. While I was watching the opening years of *Sesame Street* in the 1970s, they were becoming middle-management icons.

Grandmother. Incredible. I'm too young for gray hair and rocking chairs, so I spend my allowance on boxes of Preference by L'Oreal to avoid those annoying telltale gray strands. Then here come these little people grabbing my hand at the mall, and like a neon sign in the desert, scream out, "Grandma, Grandma," to blow my cover.

I'm irritating everyone I know with large stacks of photos of my grandsons, from the time they first opened their eyes to the present. I have a T-shirt that says "Warning, grandmother with pictures" to give strangers a chance to get out of the way before they, too, are subjected to a barrage of photos. Those boys have me gift wrapped and tied up in ribbon with their giggles and hugs.

Everything in your world changes for the better when grandchildren come into your life. What you say and do is colored in different patterns when you're a grandmother. I'm watching cartoons and videos instead of *60 Minutes*. I have reserved seating near the ball pit at McDonald's and Burger King. Even my time on the Internet has changed drastically since Joshua was born. I started looking up Disney.com and PowerRangers.com instead of the world news.

This is what I want to share with you. As a computer technician for way too many years, I want to open the world of the Internet to you—grandmother to grandmother. Do you need the Internet to be a grandmother? Of course not. Can the Internet make you a better grandmother?

Absolutely. Think of Dr. Spock, Ann Landers, Tinker Bell, and millions of other people around the world crammed into a little metal box that can sit on a table. You have access to all that knowledge and fun practically for free.

For all the "newbies" (new users) to the Web, we'll take it slow in the first chapters and then we'll build up speed. For those of you who already have played out on the World Wide Web, we'll explore some sites that you may or may not have seen in reference to your role as the grand matriarch of the family.

I want to share with you a little of my technical knowledge as well as a little of my personal experience in the magical world of the World Wide Web to enhance your role as a precious Meemaw, Nonna, or Grammie. We grandmamas need to stick together in the twenty-first century. We are the generation of maturity and familial enjoyment.

As fast as changes happen in the cyberworld, I can't guarantee that some of the Web addresses will not have changed since publication of this book. It's the nature of the virtual beast; nothing changes like cyber changes. The Internet is a communication medium, like the Pony Express or the telephone. It's a means to gather information, a tool. Knowing how to use the Internet can be fun and valuable. It provides a shared interest with your grandchildren, who will probably be cutting their teeth on computers and the Internet.

Why do you want to be out on the Internet? Because there's gold in them thar hills. It's a grandmother's cornucopia of goodies and surprises, not only for yourself but for your whole family. Wonderful nuggets of information regarding shopping, health care, and tiny tot activities are on the Internet. You want to be the grandmother that knows and shows, don't you?

The Internet holds everything from small personal Web sites created by users like yourself to highly sophisticated sites created by major companies. The volume of sites to choose from is growing daily and currently registers in the millions. As you read this book you will come across terms such as Web site, portal, and search engine. I want you to be comfortable with these terms and their differences, so I've included a description of those terms.

Web site. A Web site can be a page or a constellation of separate, but interlinked pages accessed through a homepage. Think of the homepage as the front door of a Web site. If you type my URL (Uniform Resource Locator) or Web address www.GrammaOnline.com, you will go to the home or first page of my Web site. From there you can move to a variety of different pages.

Search engine. A search engine matches the words from a search request with Web sites that it finds containing all or most of the words chosen. Let's say you want a chicken recipe. Go to a search engine such as www.Google.com and type in the words "chicken recipe" and sit back. You could spend an hour looking at the various sites that contain the words "chicken recipe."

Portal. These are more than just a Web site, and usually include some search engine capability. They offer a vast array of services and conveniences in one location. I often use www.iWon.com as a portal to news, weather, and entertainment.

"Portal" and "search engine" are not synonyms. Though portals may have search technologies, a search engine is recommended for more serious seek-and-retrieve activities on the Internet.

One last word of advice: You might sit at the computer for long periods of time. It's important to be comfortable. Let me throw in the $64,000 word: ergonomics. As defined in *Merriam-Webster's Collegiate Dictionary* ergonomics is "an applied science concerned with designing and arranging things people use so that the people and things interact most efficiently and safely." Using a computer for any length of time will start to put a strain on your hands and your neck. Be ergonomically correct—you want the top of your arms resting against the sides of your body, and the lower part of your arms straight across to the keyboard. Move around, take a break, and come back a bit later to enjoy more time at the computer.

E-mail me at grammaonline@grammaonline.com. Send me your favorite Web site or tell me about your adventures on the Internet. I'll post news and your suggestions on my Web site www.GrammaOnline.com. I hope you enjoy reading and using this book as much as I enjoyed writing it. The Internet is a fascinating place, and who should enjoy it more than us? Grandmas and fairy grandmothers are the most fascinating people I know. Combined with the Internet, we are incredible. Enjoy yourselves, Grandma said so.

CHAPTER ONE

You've Got Mail

Did you ever have a pen pal when you were a little girl? Do you remember the heart-pounding thrill of finding there was a letter for you in the mailbox when it wasn't your birthday or Christmas? Even in this techno-advanced age of Nintendo games and information super-highways, the excitement of the mailbox holding something personal hasn't changed for our grandchildren or us. The cartoon of Charlie Brown looking for a Valentine in an empty mailbox can make us all depressed.

Think of the Internet as a virtual post office. You can brighten a grandchild's day by sending them something in the mail just as they brighten yours. That feeling is universal whether we are four or eighty-four. One terrific aspect of the Internet is being able to send mail to anyone around the world for free.

Free E-mail Accounts

You are not limited to just the e-mail account with your ISP. You may set up one or more free e-mail accounts with the Internet sites listed below. (Most of the popular search engines or portals such as iWon.com or NBCi.com also offer free e-mail services.) Each account is protected by a password of your choosing so no one else can access your mail. Why would you want more than one e-mail address? Setting up an account with an Internet site assures that you can go to any computer connected to the Internet and access your e-mail at any time. Whether you are at the local library or visiting your adult children, you can access your e-mail on their computer if you are registered with a free service.

I have a separate free e-mail address that I use when I'm registering with a company on the Web if I know I'll be getting frequent notices or advertising from them. This cuts down on the amount of "spam," or junk mail, in my home inbox. I may want information about a particular company, but I don't want to search for it among personal e-mail from dear friends.

www.Hotmail.com

This is an MSN (Microsoft Network) partner and one of the world's largest providers of free e-mail services. Hotmail.com has worked to make its process easy and accessible. Once you set up your e-mail account, you can access your mail (using your private password) from any computer that has a connection to the World Wide Web. So if you're on vacation in Berlin, you can access your e-mail just as easily as if you were at home in Baltimore. Hotmail.com does not support spam or junk mail.

www.Yahoo.com

Click on Check Email and you can set up a free e-mail account. Yahoo.com offers not only their e-mail services where you can receive and send messages but also includes such additional features as a calendar and notepad. The calendar can be viewed by the month, by the week, or just one day at a time. It's a handy way to keep track of doctor appointments and special dates.

www.Juno.com

This award-winning e-mail service is now a full Internet access company. Initially Juno.com was one of the first to offer free e-mail service. It has expanded into a portal service with a variety of features on its homepage. You can set up a free e-mail account and access it anywhere. Check out JunoLand for a selection of personal user services, such as building your own Web page. Visit Juno Help to use Ask Dr. Juno to answer your questions.

www.Mail.com

Mail.com is in partnership with many leading ISP services such as Earthlink and GTE, as well as search engine and portal sites such as iWon.com. One unique feature of Mail.com is that you are not limited to using @mail.com. The second half of an e-mail address is usually the company's name, and it makes for great advertising. If you want to use whiterose as your user name, you would normally use whiterose@mail.com. At Mail.com you can select an e-mail address that fits your personality and says something about you on both sides of the @ sign. Choose from over one hundred e-mail addresses, including usa.com, europe.com, doctor.com, techie.com, engineer.com, and cheerful.com. Create an e-mail address that shows the world the real you.

www.email.com

Email.com is a service of NBCi.com, which is a partner of NBC Television. Your e-mail address would read yourname@email.com. Setting up your free e-mail account gives you all the benefits of being an NBCi.com member, such as access to local weather reports, calendar reminders, chat rooms, and personalized services available on their homepage.

E-MAIL ETIQUETTE, OR "NETIQUETTE"

Most of the rules for e-mail etiquette also pertain to other Internet activities. Together these are known as netiquette. Apply the same common courtesies to your e-mail messages that you would to a phone or face-to-face conversation. It's simply practicing good manners. For example:

Send long letters without expectations. There's nothing wrong with sending long e-mail messages informing people what you've been up to—just don't expect the same in return. Attach a P.S. to your message stating that you'd love to hear from them, but you understand they may not have the time to send a reply of similar length.

Don't SHOUT or FLAME. Do not use all capitals when typing an e-mail, posting a message, or conversing in a chat room or on a message board. This "shouting" is considered quite rude or insulting to users in the Internet world. "Flaming" is what people do when they express a strongly held opinion without holding back any emotion. It could make your reader uncomfortable.

Keep friends' e-mail addresses private. Some people are as protective of their e-mail address as they are of their home phone number and worry about it getting into the wrong hands. Delete all e-mail addresses before forwarding e-mail. Not only does this eliminate others having access to the addresses, but they won't have to scroll through a long list of names before reaching the real start of the e-mail. When sending e-mail to a group of your friends, unless they all know each other well, place your own address in the "To" box and all other addresses in the BCC (blind carbon copy) box. This feature allows the recipients to receive the e-mail with only their own address displayed.

Don't forward everything to everyone. You know your friends and family. You know what they'll appreciate and what they won't. The same joke that would leave your spouse in stitches might offend your aunt or best friend. It didn't take long before electronic mail opened up a whole new world to chain letters. These are not the kind where you send a dishtowel to the name on top of the list and add yours to the bottom. They are more likely a poem or a piece of prose, and down at the bottom it promises good luck if you forward it to five or more of your friends. You do not have to send them on; the computer fairies will thank you for not clogging the Net with more junk mail.

Don't forward invitations. If you receive an invitation to a party via e-mail, do not forward the message to others. Instead, ask the people hosting the party if they mind if you bring along a few friends. After all, it is their party, not yours.

Remember tone is lost in e-mail. Even when sending quick e-mail messages to friends, remember that it's almost impossible to capture tone and attitude the way you can in a phone conversation. The reader could interpret an innocent comment sent in jest as rude. Make sure that your messages are clear, and avoid using sarcasm. Or add an emoticon (a smiley face) or acronym like LOL (laughing out loud) to show your feelings. We'll talk about emoticons and acronyms later in this chapter.

Don't be a spoiler. Sure, it's nice to know the outcome of your favorite TV show's cliffhanger ending or the plot twist to the latest movie before everyone else. Just keep in mind that not all of your friends or relatives will appreciate having you reveal these secrets. Send any potentially plot-revealing e-mail with "Warning! This e-mail contains spoiler information about [subject matter]," in the subject box. Those who want to remain in suspense can simply delete the e-mail without reading it.

Beware of hoaxes. Most e-mail messages and e-mail users are sincere and mean you no harm. However, if you receive a message from someone whose name is unfamiliar to you, do not reply. It may be a salesperson or someone trying to scam you. You may also receive incredible messages forwarded by your friends, that claim some company will pay you money if you forward this e-mail to others. Wrong. Just as Bill Gates of Microsoft will not pay anyone for each e-mail forwarded, neither is there someone that paid $250 for a cookie recipe, and no one earns a car if you keep the chain mail going. These myths are annoying. No one can track a forwarded e-mail. Do everyone a favor and delete these. Stop the insanity.

If you receive a message warning of a new computer virus, or that a certain product contains poison, or your favorite TV show is being canceled for blatant reasons, confirm the e-mail before forwarding to all of your friends. I cannot tell you how rampant some people's imaginations are. They will create the most asinine e-mail and forward it with a plea begging the recipients to forward it to everyone they know. Check out www.UrbanLegends.com for information on any e-mail that seems suspicious or strange to you.

COMPUTERESE

Acronyms that are used in e-mail messages and chat rooms are called "computerese," a form of e-mail short-hand. You do not have to use them; they just cut down on the amount of typing.

BBL—Be back later
BFN—Bye for now
BTW—By the way
CUL8R—See you later
CYA—See ya
FYI—For your information
HTH—Hope this helps
IOW—In other words
IMHO—In my humble opinion
LOL—Laughing out loud
NRN—No reply necessary
ROTFL—Rolling on the floor laughing
TY—Thank you
YW—You're welcome

WRT—With respect to
Zzzzz—Boring
<g>—Grinning
{} or ( )—hug

Emoticons (expressive icons) can also be used to display an emotion in your typing.

:-) —happy face
:-(—sad face
;-) —winking face
:-D —laughing face
:-o —surprised or shocked face

E-Greeting Cards

Once you feel comfortable sending your grandchildren and friends notes by e-mail, you are ready for the next great adventure: greeting cards. Electronic greeting cards are quick, free, and entertaining. E-greetings have become a popular staple of Net users. These are not just splashes of color and design; you can add the child's name and usually type a personalized greeting of 250 characters (letters and numbers), which is quite a bit. Some e-greetings are animated cartoons. Others include a bit of instrumental background music or sound effects.

There are many Web sites that offer electronic greeting cards and postcards. In some cases, greeting cards may only be a portion of their services, as with search engines like www.Yahoo.com and www.iWon.com. When you visit a Web site, look around the top of the homepage or on the sidebars to see if it offers free e-greetings. Even the Tylenol people have put free e-mail cards on their Web site. They call them Care Cards. Send a Care Card to someone you care about with a *Touched by an Angel* theme.

Any and every major holiday will be listed. I even believe some of these sites make up a few "holidays" each month to encourage use of their greeting cards—holidays like Chocolate Chip Day or Men-Have-to-Make-Dinner day. Did you know you can send a greeting card celebrating May 10, the anniversary of the completion of the transcontinental railroad? Don't forget the second Sunday of September is Grandparents Day. Check these sites often for ideas.

www.BlueMountain.com

BlueMountain.com offers a friendly site with e-greeting options broken up into sections such as Stay In Touch or Events & Milestones. The homepage shows you holidays and significant events for the current month. These are listed on the left side for easy perusing. Just below the current calendar you'll find their out-of-season calendar where you can look to see what's coming up. Greetings in languages other than English are available. Blue-Mountain.com also offers other features such as free e-mail (through Excite.com).

www.Bowcreek.com

Four hundred different postcards in a variety of categories are available to you at Bowcreek.com. Each can be personalized and e-mailed to friends and family. Once you've picked your card design, you have the options of adding musical backgrounds, changing the color of the text, or adding a bit of poetry. Just click on your choices and hit the Preview button to see your card before sending it out. Go back and edit or change any of your selections if you'd like, then click Send.

www.4-evercards.com

Based out of Wisconsin, this is a great e-greeting Web site created and maintained by just two people, Ktoon and Gazoo. 4-evercards.com is dedicated to creating the best family-friendly site of free postcards on the Net. Easy-to-use, drop-down menus guide you when you choose a category. For example, under Animals and Pets, you'll find Woobie Wishes. Under General and Humor you have Men Sucking Up cards. (Now if we could just get them to use these cards.) Most important, be sure to check out the Grand-Greetings section under the category Relationships. You'll find beautifully drawn e-greeting cards of grandparents available, inspired by *moi*. Ktoon is a professional cartoonist and she designs most of the postcards. Gazoo is the Web site's techie. You'll love the many other special features and links this site holds as well. Mark this as a Favorite so you can return to it easily.

www.123greetings.com

123greetings.com has a wonderful selection of cards. Imagination runs high on this Web site, and it offers lots of inventive reasons for sending a card to someone. Most of the graphics on the homepage are animated, giving it an entertaining feel. Check out the Events and Holidays section for a list of ideas for card giving during the current month.

www.AmericanGreetings.com

American Greetings has their own Web site of e-greeting cards with all the quality you've come to associate with them. Not only do they have an extensive selection of online greetings, they also have cards you can print out yourself if you have a color printer at home. Check out the Create and Print section. It's easy to make up greeting cards you can then send through snail mail. Best of all, it's free.

www.Hallmark.com

The Hallmark site features specialty character cards such as their own Maxine. (I'm beginning to look more and more like her as time goes on, though I don't own a pair of bunny slippers.) Hallmark.com also includes such personal services as an address book for your favorite friends' e-mail addresses and a calendar for their birthdays and anniversaries. Both make the process of sending a card much easier.

www.eGreetings.com

Send a video greeting card to your best friend with boy band 98° serenading her and I'll guarantee it'll bring a smile to her face. Many cards are animated. Become a member—it's free—and see new card selections before anyone else.

www.Regards.com

Regards.com offers more than 5,000 cards in 150 content categories. They have evolved into a one-stop communication site with features that include reminder services for important dates such as birthdays and anniversaries, chat rooms, and even a print service where you can order personalized mailing labels or stationery.

www.Blab.com

Blab.com has more than just quality animated greeting cards for any occasion. Click on Calendar for a delightful look at upcoming events. Register as a member and take advantage of Reminder Services for those key dates in your life. Greeting cards are even available in fourteen different languages. *Ciao, Bella.*

www.1001BestGreetings.com

What a collection of cards and ideas to choose from! If it can't be found here, it probably doesn't exist. But if no one else makes it, you always can. Click on Custom Greetings and make up your own e-greetings. Pick a background design, stamp, poem, music, and more. New imaginative e-greetings are added every week.

Message Boards, Chat Rooms, and Mailing Lists

Want to e-mail other grandparents? Do you have questions or concerns only another grandmother would be able to understand? It may be time for you to take advantage of message boards, particularly those available at Web sites that focus on grandparents and grandparenting. Message boards are similar to writing and sending e-mail messages but the messages are posted in a central area, not an individual mailbox. Topics on a grandparenting site might include First-Time Grandmother, Grandparent Visitation Rights, or How Do You Stay in Touch with Long-Distance Grandchildren. Lists of topics and their responses are shown for you to scan through. A user writes a message or asks a question at a message board and this posts to a list. Anyone who finds the topic or lead words interesting can open it and read or reply to it. This new message is then available for others to read and/or respond to.

A message board enables you to post a question or a thought that will be seen by thousands of people visiting this same area. You can also reply to something you may have read on the message board. You can find specialty message boards or discussion groups at many of the major Web sites.

Chat rooms enable you to have a written conversation with other people in real time. You may feel a bit confused the first few times you visit a chat room, as there may be many chats going on at the same time. Because of this, you may want to "lurk before you leap," meaning you may want to read some of the dialogue—to see if you can follow a conversation and to determine if these are people with whom you want to talk—before you join the conversations.

How does a chat room work? You are sending short, brief e-mails to a central location that prints your statements or questions as soon as you hit Enter. Other people in the chat room are doing the same. Meanwhile the messages are scrolling upwards in a window on your screen as new dialogue is added to the chat room. When you first enter, you may feel like an intruder. Most senior-related chat rooms, though, include friendly users that will encourage you to join in.

In chat rooms topics may be about anything and everything, with three or four conversations going at the same time. Some Web sites have only a main chat room, others may break out topic matters into separate rooms such as Trivia or Current Events.

If you want scores of e-mail, join a mailing list. The purpose of most lists is to send out news updates or talk about a specific topic. What areas interest you the most? Topics range from cars, children, health, pets, or senior issues to many more. Perhaps you're an animal lover. There are hundreds of mailing lists that relate to animals, but you might want to be more specific. A search on cats will still leave you with over a hundred to choose from and be happy with. If you are a fan of Scottish Folds or Himalayans, there are mailing lists just for you.

Mailing lists are like a centralized mailbox: If you post something, it will be delivered by e-mail to everyone on the list. "Discussions" are held by exchanging e-mails. Mailing lists are an easy way to stay on top of news on a particular topic or meet people with a similar interest. Joining a mailing list is usually simple: You fill out a form on a Web site or send a single e-mail message requesting to join. Keep the first welcome message, as it usually tells you how to "unsubscribe" (i.e., have your name removed) from the list as well.

www.iGrandparents.com

This is a wonderful Web site just for grandparents; it was set up by grandparents. Check out its list of Grand Topics, the informational sections, the gift baskets, the contests, and more. Click on Community and you'll find their message boards and chat rooms where you can contact other grandparents with your questions and concerns or to share a story of your own. Grandma Betty's Corner, where you will find a variety of Web site links with grandparents in mind, is a must. You'll find a chat room for Grandma Betty's fans and friends. Stop in and say hello.

www.GrandparentWorld.com

This colorful site offers many features including a message board section where you can share a story, ask a question, or just interact with other grandparents. Also check out Soup, where you find a page in the form of a soup pot filled with tidbits, stories, and more.

www.GrandsPlace.com

This is a Web site for grandparents and special others that are raising grandchildren. Find resources and information as well as message boards; take advantage of GrandsPlace

Chat. This site also offers a free newsletter. If you'd like to sign up for that, it will be delivered twice a month to your e-mail inbox.

www.EssentialGrandparent.com

Check out Dr. Lillian Carson's Web site regarding her books and advice on grandparenting. Dr. Carson is a nationally renowned authority on child development, parenting, and grandparenting. She was named McGrandMom for McDonald's. Click on TEG Reading Circle or the questions and answers section, where you have a chance to ask Dr. Carson about your concerns regarding grandparenting.

www.Topica.com

This is a cornucopia of information resources including e-mail lists to which you may wish to add your name to receive updates on particular topics. You can browse its best categories, or go into its Informative Newsletter section. You can click on Hot Topics and then choose from Breaking News, Cool Web Sites, Health, or Sports. Topica.com makes the sign-up process simple whether you're a first-time user or an expert.

www.CoolList.com

This is an easy-to-use site for mailing lists. Keep in touch with others with similar interests by subscribing to particular lists such as Arts & Entertainment, Shopping, or World. You may only join public lists unless invited to join a private list. CoolList.com allows members to create their own lists; some are by invitation only. To subscribe to a public list, just click on Join a New List at the menu bar located at the top of the page. Type the name of the list in the first box and your e-mail address on the next line. A confirmation e-mail will be sent to you to confirm your subscription.

Groups.Yahoo.com

This is a free e-mail group service that allows you to easily create and join e-mail groups. Under its section Join a Group, Yahoo! Groups offers a convenient way to connect with others who share the same interests and ideas. Find a collection of headings to choose from. Click on Cultures & Community, click on Groups, and you'll find a list of subheadings, including Seniors. Click on Seniors, where you will find even more options and groups from which to choose.

DAILY E-MAIL SITES

You can sign up at various Web sites for daily e-mail doses of jokes, inspirational sayings, positive quotes of the day, and more. Are you a trivia buff? You can sign up for a daily e-mail trivia. Want to see your horoscope every morning? There is no end of information you can receive. Various sites, such as the ones given below, offer lists of possible items you can receive every day. Just register and choose the subjects you most want to see.

www.EMAZING.com

This is a user-friendly site filled with sections such as Brain Candy, which includes Fortune Cookies and Famous Birthdays, or Household Hints, which includes Domestic Goddess, Cats, and Cooking. The Daybreakers section offers news information and more. Click on the boxes of the items you would like to receive and sign up using your e-mail address. It's that simple.

www.MailBits.com

MailBits.com is set up to deliver snippets of the Internet to you. Sign up for a daily delivery of trivia, jokes, famous quotes, and freebies from the site. Or click on Customized and choose from a large selection of topics. MailBits.com will then send you bits of up-to-date information or little-known offers relating to your choices.

www.KidsLoveMail.com

This wonderful site offers memberships in various "clubs," from which you can purchase different mailings for your grandchildren. The site includes sticker and stationery clubs where you can purchase products that will be sent periodically through the mail, gift card included, to your special grandchild. KidsLoveMail.com sticker collections include famous cartoon characters from Disney, Barbie, Hot Wheels, and more. Ordering is all done right at the computer, and you don't have to do anything but provide the information. Buy a stationery packet for your grandchildren and encourage them to write to you, other relatives, and their friends. Get them in the habit of sharing their thoughts on paper.

www.ListFarm.com

ListFarm.com, a daily e-mail site, has eight sections to peruse. Or click on View All Lists and see everything at once. Make your choices and register with your e-mail address. You will be sent a confirmation e-mail to which you must respond in order to begin your daily subscription.

The more you reach out, whether it is through electronic mail or the old snail mail process, the more you'll get back in return. There is a world out there waiting to hear what you have to say—a world containing little branches of your family tree that adore anything and everything you send them as their Nonna or their Meemaw, a world containing other grandmothers who have the same question, or had the same experience as you had, and would love to share thoughts with you.

Once you enter a Web site for women such as www.iVillage.com or one for grandparents such as www.iGrandparents.com, you have the opportunity to correspond with people all over the United States and around the world. Don't sit quietly and read about other women's lives, join in. You have stories that will bring a smile to someone you've never met and concerns that others will understand.

Join in and your mailbox will never be empty again.

Cyber Shop Till You Drop

Cyber shopping from a computer has incredible advantages over regular drive-to-the-mall kind of shopping. There's no traffic to fight, no driving up and down the aisles of a parking lot trying to find an empty space within half a mile of the store. It doesn't matter if it's raining outside or if a blinding snowstorm is raging because your shopping is going to be done in the comfort of your own home.

The Internet is open twenty-four hours a day, seven days a week. If you want to order the latest Barbie doll as a birthday present for your granddaughter at five in the morning, you go, girl. You don't have to get dressed up and brush your hair to cyber shop. If you want to order Christmas presents in your chenille bathrobe and slippers after the evening news in August, you go right ahead. Can shopping get any better than this?

Quick, convenient, and secure: Shopping online is no more than ordering your heart's desires from a Web site with a click of the mouse on the item or items, then a few keystrokes for typing in your name, shipping and billing addresses, and credit card information.

Most of the larger corporate sites have a "shopping cart." You select an item by clicking it with your mouse, and it is placed in your shopping cart. The screen then shows the "contents" of your cart, indicating the item you just selected. It shows the quantity as "one"; you can change the quantity if necessary. You're then asked if you'd like to continue shopping or head for the checkout. Let's head for the checkout. You're asked for a shipping address (you can have it mailed directly to your grandchild if you'd like) and a billing address.

Next it will ask for your credit card information. (Is it safe to type your credit card information into the computer? Yes, it's just as safe as if you were in a store and handing your card to a clerk.) You will see in the text or fine print on the screen that the payment information is in a secured, encoded area. You may even see a small yellow padlock on the screen to reassure you that this is a secured area. You've probably heard horror stories of someone getting a credit card number and using it fraudulently, but it's not usually from Internet use. (However, always check your credit card billing statement each month, even if you never use a credit card on the Internet. It's a sound business habit.)

You have one last chance to check your information on the items, the quantity, and the shipping address before you push the button to purchase. You will get a confirmation screen that you can print out or an e-mail telling you that your purchase request was accepted and is being processed. In a few days, depending on the items you've ordered and their availability, the package arrives at the door by U.S. Postal Service, UPS, or some other delivery service. No muss, no fuss.

Though online shopping is quick, convenient, and safe, please remember that this chapter comes with a warning label. By listing shopping sites, I am not encouraging you to go into debt. If you get too excited with your purchasing power out on the Web, you won't be facing cyber debt or "virtual" debt but tried and true credit card debt.

Shopping online is not like walking through a regular mall where your legs get tired and the handles of bags start cutting the circulation off in both arms so you know you've spent a lot of money. Those physical aches and pains are quick notes to your brain that you should stop spending and go home. There are no aching legs, numb arms, or shopping police to warn you of overspending on the Internet.

If you lust after those bargains that you find at the back of a sales rack, or if you love pawing over tables filled with discontinued items trying to find one that has all its parts, cyber shopping can still satisfy that clearance-sale hunger. Most sites have a bargain or discount section, and if that's not enough for you, wait until you see the auction Web sites. Promotion coupons like ten dollars off your first order are also prolific on the Internet.

You will not live by cyber shopping alone. Shopping on the Internet just makes life a little easier and you can't do better than that some days.

Auctions

Auction sites are a great place to find new and used items. Think of them as giant global garage sales or swap meets filled with a variety of the past and the present. You can find collectibles, antiques, and more. Each item comes with a minimum bid and posts how long the item will be up for auction. You can spend hours looking through the sections.

There is a certain amount of risk as to what you may be bidding on, and not all sellers will provide a photo of the item or detailed description. You should approach these purchases with a "buyer beware" attitude.

www.eBay.com

eBay.com is the world's largest personal online trading site. It offers efficient one-to-one trading in an auction bid format on the Web. Currently it has over four thousand categories and millions of items to bid for. Buying or selling items on eBay.com is relatively simple; just follow the instructions given on the site. Rosie O'Donnell has her own section of celebrity-autographed items from guests on her talk show she posts on eBay.com. All the money raised goes to her For All Kids Foundation.

www.uBid.com

This site offers consumers and small- to medium-sized businesses a chance to designate their price in purchasing name-brand merchandise in a secure, reliable auction site. uBid.com features a daily rotating selection of more than 6,700 name-brand products in more than twelve different categories including computers, monitors and printers, consumer electronics, apparel, home and leisure, art, home improvement, travel and events, major appliances, jewelry and gifts, and sports and recreation.

www.FirstAuction.com

Here you will find the unique feature known as "flash" auctions. These thirty-minute special auctions are posted twenty times a day and feature an assortment of items from computer equipment to jewelry. On the drop-down menu, you can click on Find a Flash drop-down menu and choose a time you know you'll be at your computer to see what will be up for bid.

www.Christies.com

The world-famous London auction house is now online. While it is known for international glamour and selling high-priced works of art, many of the items offered at Christies.com are affordable to even novice collectors. There are hundreds of auctions throughout the year at which objects of every description for aspiring collectors, homemakers, and people simply looking to buy some-thing distinctive are sold. Featured auctions and events are listed on the homepage as is an auction calendar where you can check to see what kind and where the auc-tions will be held.

www.eWanted.com

This is a new twist to the online auction idea. You post an item that you are looking for, with an amount you would like to pay for it, and sellers will contact you. This eliminates hours of searching through various auction sites. eWanted.com has over a thousand categories and subcategories of items and services. All you do is register, click on Make A Request, and enter what it is that you are trying to find. eWanted.com will provide a secure system to get what you want.

www.InternetAuctionList.com

This is a portal to auction sites. Why go through each individual auction site when you can do a search for a par-ticular item through many sites all at once? InternetAuc-tionList.com (IAL) compiles up-to-date information on items being sold at approximately 150 different online auction sites, thus providing a search on over five million total items. Your search for an antique rocking horse or a fifteen-inch computer monitor will result in a thorough list of items. The search results will give you the site name, current bid, time it will close as well as a direct link to the auction item itself. You can also set up an Alert Me Daily for an item, where IAL will e-mail you a listing that fits the item you're looking for.

THE POWER OF THE INTERNET

It was 1999 and my soon-to-be-five-year-old grandson's hero of the moment was the White Ranger of the Mighty Morphin Power Rangers, circa 1994–95. His interest was due to reruns on TV. Okay, I admit I was partially responsible for creating this post-Morphin passion through some used videos I had gotten. Now Joshua wanted a Power Ranger birthday party.

The rest of his generation was into *Star Wars: The Phantom Menace* and the Pokemon craze. I could find nothing for Mighty Morphin Power Rangers. This is where the Internet came to the rescue. I logged onto www.eBay.com and typed Mighty Morphin Power Rangers in the window box and clicked Search. What came up here: hundreds, probably a thousand items that people had for sale about the Power Rangers. Did I care why? No, I was grateful.

I made bids and was highest bidder on a complete set of paper products, including plates, cups, and napkins for Joshua's party. The power of Internet purchasing didn't stop there, as I found decorative banners and plastic tablecloths. Did I walk away from the computer? No. I kept going back to eBay.com and found a person auctioning six life-sized cardboard cutouts of the Rangers, two of which were of Tommy, the White Ranger. I picked up the whole set for less than five dollars a piece.

Not only were my grandson and his friends in awe at his party, but I also had parents come up and ask where I had found the decorations. We took photos of each child standing next to a Power Ranger cutout as a souvenir. It wouldn't have been the successful Power Ranger party it was without auction site shopping.

The power of the Internet added to the power of being a grandmother equals magic in the eyes of grandchildren when you can make a dream like that come true.

Apparel

How many of us have an aversion to fitting rooms? You try something on in this tiny booth with bright fluorescent lights surrounded by mirrors; you take it off. You try on something else; you take it off. Is there a better way? Wouldn't it be great to type in all your necessary body dimensions and find something that fits and looks great? You can on the Internet. What about personal service, someone to pick out your clothes? That's out there too.

You can do a search for clothing, women's or children's, and spend time perusing the different sites and items, much as you would during a day of shopping in the real world—without the hassles of parking the car and walking everywhere. What if you're looking for something in particular, such as a basic black dress for the holidays or a sweater coat to wear on your next vacation? The Internet has "shop bots" out there: cyber-shopping Web sites that will go out and search other sites for the best price of a particular item and report back to you.

www.Target.com

The one and only store with the red-and-white bull's-eye logo is online. You can click on Clothing, Women's, and pick a designer like Cherokee to view their offerings. Click on Sizing, and Target.com will give you a complete chart on waist, hip, and bust measurements for various styles—no more searching through the rack and not finding your size. Order it online.

www.LaneBryant.com

LaneBryant.com has an outfit generator process where you can mix and match over three thousand different outfit combinations. Use your imagination. It's your chance to create the ultimate outfit. Or consult their Style Guru. After you answer a few questions about your tastes, the guru of LaneBryant.com will pull up samples for you.

www.Talbots.com

Known for their fifty years of quality stores and catalog business, Talbot.com offers women's and children's apparel in a variety of categories. Click on the sales icon in each section for their latest selections. Click on Style Guide for a fashion show in slides.

www.Gap.com

Here's something for the whole family. The famous Gap casual wear can be found online for both men and women's fashions. Click on Baby Gap to see the latest selections in newborn to toddler size. Click on Gap Kids for selections in girls' and boys' wear. Hassle-free returns are promised if something doesn't fit right. You can return it to any Gap store location—they provide a list of addresses—or by mail.

www.StoreRunner.com

StoreRunner.com allows you one-stop convenience instead of searching for an item at a variety of Web sites. Type in a keyword, such as red sweater, and within seconds you will see a list of sites. You can narrow your search by price, by store, and even by location with just a click on the screen. Easy-to-use directions allow you to store items on a wish list if you're not ready to purchase but want to keep track of the items. StoreRunner.com is a CBS alliance company.

www.TheSockCompany.com

Here is a place full of warm fuzzies and undergarments. Check out the large supply of brand names—such as Morgan, Russell, Champion—in sweats, thermals, and more. You'll find socks of every variety imaginable from athletic socks to odor eaters, baby socks to dress socks. Click on Hot Sox to see offers of toe socks and patterns to delight anyone on a special occasion or holiday.

www.GrandmaU.com

You have to check this out. It's a darling Web site of logo sweatshirts and T-shirts from the Grandma University campus gift shop. "Grandma University, The Halls of Higher Hugging" is its motto. Click on Facts & Philosophies to learn that not all grandchildren are created equal. Yours are cuter and smarter. Another "fact" about G.U. coeds is that not only do they act and think young, they actually look much younger than their real age. This is backed up by countless studies conducted by the unbiased student body, both with and without their glasses on. Click on Newsletter for more smiles. Check out the colors and patterns of G.U. women's wear. Future updates to this site will include many additional features. Come back often.

www.BabyTees.com

Offers a variety of infant and toddler wear with colorful and adorable sayings by Rein Designs, Inc. Click on the Grandma Package or the Grandpa Package and see a selection of bibs and onesies to make you smile. Size information is available for ordering the one-piece suits. Be sure to register for e-mail specials.

www.LandsEnd.com

Click on Personal Model and build a 3-D replica with your specific body measurements. Try different clothes and outfits on your own virtual model and see how they look—even the dreaded bathing suits. Let your personal model do all the embarrassing work for you and save you from breaking out in a cold sweat. Click on My Personal Shopper for the feeling of having your own wardrobe consultant.

www.PurpleSkirt.com

Famous television personality Tracey Ullman is behind this Web site of quality women's clothing and accessories. Click on My Closet and set up your own profile where site stylists will pick out items you might like and keep you posted on new items in stock. Designer names are carried for a higher quality inventory, such as Lily Cheung, Isadora Story, and Diane von Furstenberg. Prices for many items are in the three-figure range.

I bought my first grandson a Baby Morgan brand white receiving blanket that had an inch of silk binding material around the edges. I got it at Wal-Mart. That little piece of fabric became the blankie, the don't-go-anywhere-without-it blanket.

When I went back to buy another Baby Morgan, none of my local stores carried them any longer. What's a desperate grandmother to do? How many guessed on the first try? That's right, I went to the Internet and did a search on Baby Morgan blankets. Not only did I find www.TheSockCompany.com carried Baby Morgan receiving blankets in a variety of colors, but they were also cheaper than what I originally paid. The Sock Company also sold mini Baby Morgan receiving blankets, same exact blanket, but in doll size. How cute is that? Did Gramma buy a few? You bet I did.

Automobiles

Yes, you can buy a car on the Internet. Sounds incredible, I know. Slick new models are paraded in color and detailed specifications are given at the Web sites of vehicle manufacturers. You can also find used automobiles, some with limited warranties, on various Web sites. This is the ultimate in car shopping for me. No hopping from car lot to car lot and no salesperson pressuring you to make a decision. I like the idea of being able to look at any car style and see what options are available (I have to have air conditioning) and an approximate price for it. Granted, you can't test-drive a car on the Internet, but, when you're ready to make a decision, you can go down to a dealer fully prepared to get the most for your money.

www.Toyota.com

From Avalon to Tundra, you can click on a Toyota model and see a variety of information at your fingertips. My personal favorite is the RAV4. Click on specifications to find out interior dimensions, gas mileage, and more. There are also sections on this site for financing, insurance, and dealer location.

www.GMC.com

GMC.com lists a complete selection of trucks, vans, and SUVs with just a click of your mouse. Want information about dealers? Click on the icon. Brochure information for each of the models from the Envoy to Yukon is available. Room, style, and comfort are given in the breakdown with each vehicle.

www.Ford.com

You can click on Ford's online showroom for new cars and models, or you can click on preowned selections, backed by the Ford Motor Company with a 100-point inspection. You can choose from small or midsize, sports or luxury cars, to convertibles or minivans. Custom build your own Lincoln, Volvo, Jaguar, or Mazda vehicle. Click on Dealership information for locations near you. See Special Buying Programs for purchase plans such as Youth Driver Education and Mobility Monitoring Program.

www.iMotors.com

iMotors.com handles used cars, one to five years old. Search for the make and model of the car of your choice. They will locate it, check it out with their service department, and deliver it to you or the nearest iMotor.com center. Every iMotors.com vehicle must pass a rigorous 269-point certification process including diagnostic testing, preventative maintenance, and cosmetic care. Purchase of an iMotors.com vehicle includes a 7-day/700-mile money back return policy and a 3-month/3,000-mile warranty.

www.CarsDirect.com

Type in a make of car, select a model, and enter your zip code. CarsDirect.com will instantly locate information on the car of your choice and display an easy-to-read list of options. You pick and choose what options you'd like on the car, and a price breakdown of each of those options appears on the right side of your screen. At the top of the screen, you will see the list price, the total price, and an average monthly lease or loan payment. I chose a RAV4 with options and within seconds I had the information I wanted.

www.Vehix.com

This is a third-party service on the Net that can help you learn about safety ratings of a particular model or Kelley Blue Book information. Build your ideal car with their easy-to-use custom tables showing makes, models, options, paint, and trim. Learn how to take care of your car, how to purchase and sell cars, and how to control the cost of owning a car. Find information on a variety of topics, including loans, lease options, and insurance deals.

www.Autoweb.com

Another multilayered Web site, Autoweb.com locates information on new or used cars. Features include sections on research and buying a car, auto maintenance, finance and insurance, and selling your current car. Autoweb.com is an iWon.com alliance with CBS.

www.KBB.com

Want to know what your current car is worth? Looking to buy a used car? Go to the official Kelley Blue Book site and click on the Used Car Value link. Type in the make and model of your car and what type of shape you feel it is in. A report will automatically come up on your screen.

This site can also help you with referral services with links to automobile Web sites for buying a new or used car. This is useful as well if you are thinking of donating your current car to a local charity. Use the Kelley Blue Book information to see what your car's current value might be and print a copy for your tax records.

www.Edmunds.com

Offers advice on pricing, buying, and financing your new or used car. Use their Frequently Asked Questions section to find a wealth of information such as "How do I figure a fair deal?" Edmund's Reviews of each make and model can be invaluable in shopping around for a new car.

Books

Even in this day of high-tech gadgetry, there is nothing like curling up on the couch with a good book— especially on a cool, wet afternoon with a cup of tea. You can find a selection of online bookstores to boggle the mind of any reader. Check out a publisher's Web site to find out what new books by your favorite authors will be coming out. Some authors are posting their own personal stories and background information on the Internet. Do a search for your favorite authors and see what's new and upcoming from them. You can also post book reviews at some of the major bookstores.

www.Amazon.com

One of the original online bookstores, Amazon.com opened its virtual doors in 1995 with a goal to use the Internet to transform book buying into the fastest, easiest, and most enjoyable shopping experience possible. Once your account is set up with Amazon.com, you have the convenience of "One-Click" shopping. Choose a book from the millions of selections, then with one click of your mouse it will be processed and mailed to you directly. Amazon.com also offers a plethora of other merchandise such as videos, music, and more.

www.Alibris.com

Shop for books you thought you'd never find. Alibris.com has an inventory of thousands of booksellers that you can access from one secure and reliable source. Find a book and they'll retrieve it, whether it's from a tiny Alaskan bookshop or plucked from their own warehouse shelves. You have access to a database of millions of hard-to-find books, manuscripts, photos, and autographs.

www.bn.com

This is the national bookstore, Barnes & Noble, online. You will find sections for rare and out-of-print books, music, videos, and more. Click on Magazine Store to find over one thousand magazines to which you can subscribe. Click on Chats and Events for possible interviews with your favorite author. Bn.com has a directory of their store locations and an activity roster for most of the upcoming special events at each store.

www.TatteredCover.com

This independent online bookstore carries an extensive inventory of assorted titles in new books. Join their Autographed Book Club and each month you will receive one autographed first edition of a book chosen by the Tattered Cover staff. Selections include both fiction and nonfiction.

www.TenSpeed.com

Ten Speed Press is the publisher for *Grandma Online* as well as many other great nonfiction books. Check out the selection of their award-winning cookbooks. Click on Kid Zone and see what Tricycle Press has coming out in children's books. All Products under Catalog will let you scroll through the book titles of any or all divisions.

www.Powells.com

How would you like to visit the world's largest new and used bookstore without ever leaving home? Do the Shuffle, the Powell's Shuffle under their Browse section. At Powell's Bookstore you'll find used books are shelved right next to new copies of the same titles. At Powells.com you can do a search of used titles—simply use their checkbox function. You don't want to miss any of the other great features of this site, such as the Book Talk Café. Plan on staying a while.

www.bibliofind.com

Here is where you can find more than 20 million used and rare books offered for sale by thousands of booksellers from all over the world in one easy location. Looking for a specific issue of *Life* magazine? You can find periodicals for sale on this site as well. Type in *Life* magazine in the Title search box and a list will come up with dates and descriptions of each available copy. Shopping Cart convenience is available.

Collectibles

For those with a knickknack shelf filled with salt and pepper shakers of various characters or a curio cabinet with antique dolls, here are some Web sites for expanding your collection with hard-to-find items from the comfort of your own home. No longer will you have to drive to various thrift stores and hole-in-the-wall antique shops where you only find a treasure once in a while. You can look once a week or every day online.

Many of the larger portal sites have a collectibles section in their features. The sites below list their wares and information for you in color right on your computer.

Find out interesting details, meet people that enjoy the same collectibles as you, and have fun.

www.UniqueCollectibles.com

This is one of the best sites in entertainment and sports collectibles. It has a large selection of autographs, posters, photos, and collectibles of your favorite stars or casts in movies or television. Its homepage employs easy-to-use categories of Sports, Music, and Movie & TV to start your browsing. UniqueCollectibles.com takes pride in the fifteen customer service awards acquired from various hobby publications over the years. E-Entertainment Television, the *New York Times*, and the *Los Angeles Times* have featured the company as an authority for the industry.

www.CollectiblesToday.com

This is the Web division of The Bradford Group, a leading international provider of limited-edition collectibles. Enjoy not only artwork from The Bradford Group companies but also many others such as Disney, Department 56, Hummel, Thomas Kinkade, and more. With one click you can browse the list of categories by brand name or by form/theme. This quality site offers a full one-year money-back guarantee (including postage) for any item bought, for any reason. Click on

News/Forums. Newsstand offers information regarding artists and collectibles, while at Forum you can talk with other collectors by posting on their message boards.

www.PeterandMark.com

Two collectors, Peter Linski and Mark McMahon, have put their catalog of Pez dispensers, cookie jars, ceramic banks, salt and pepper shakers, and toys online. Click on Search and do a one-word search through their eclectic inventory.

www.2oldshoppinbags.com

Step into the past with this delightful site. Just the name itself is perfect, don't you think? Click on the word Catalog to see its categories of fun and antique items. You can choose from The General Store, Items From Around the House, The Knick-Knack Shelf, and more. You can click on Current eBay Auctions, which will take you to the site's list of items currently up for bid on eBay.com.

www.MouseMan.com

Could you guess this is a Disneyana collectors' site? Bob Crooker has put his catalog of collectible Disney items online for your convenience. Check out the main menu and note that you can click on the current online items for sale or on previews of upcoming items. The quality and age of these items is excellent. It's worth stopping just to take a look at the photographs of the items available.

www.Collectibles.com

Collectibles.com is the online companion for Shop At Home, Inc., a televised shopping service. Shop At Home has taken its vast inventory of collectible items as well as its quality customer service to the Internet. You can do a search with a keyword or two, or just browse through the many categories listed for your pleasure.

www.RubyLane.com

Visit this one-stop, easy-to-use online resource for finding, buying, and selling antiques, collectibles, and fine art. Set up like a courtyard of shops in old New Orleans, you can search and browse through detailed categories and selections. Or do a search on a keyword and Ruby-Lane.com will bring up its list of items available.

www.icsNOW.com

icsNOW.com is the online connection to the International Collectors Society. They use their expertise to search the world of the most desirable limited-edition items of favorite people, places, and events. Membership is free. You can acquire CollectorPoints, which you can use toward future purchases, for every collectible purchase made on this site.

What a cornucopia of character items—both old and new! The homepage offers an easy-to-search Favorites section with names from Batman to the Wizard of Oz, and from Heckle and Jeckle to Hello Kitty. Refrigerator magnets, coffee mugs, and more are available. Note: They do have a Dangerous Attitude section with more mature audience in mind—nothing risqué, but grand-parental guidance may be necessary.

Music and Videos

Is there anything more soothing than a memorable ballad like "Tara's Theme" from *Gone with the Wind* or anything more suspenseful than an old Hitchcock film? Music and film enrich our lives in many ways. They enlighten, engage, and entertain us. We see the same appreciation in our grandchildren's faces as they watch a favorite video for the tenth time and ask you to play it again.

Sometimes we want to hear a new song or the grand-children want to see a new film just released on video; at other times we want to wrap ourselves up in a favorite oldie. Help the younger generations appreciate the black-and-white classics with Cary Grant or Katharine Hepburn, or both in the movie *Bringing Up Baby*.

Whatever music or video you're looking for, you can probably find it on the Web.

www.CDNOW.com

Browse through the categories of music or videos to find your favorites. You can also make your own custom CD by picking any twelve songs from CDNOW's inventory. Create a wedding CD for someone, or put your grandchild's favorite music hits together on one CD as a special holiday gift. Let your grandchildren create a Wish List of their favorite artists so you know who's going to make them happy at birthday time. Subscribe to its services and CDNOW.com will send you e-mail notices on upcoming sales as well as information regarding your favorite artists.

www.TowerRecords.com

TowerRecord.com's homepage is easy to use. Just click on Music to enter the online music store. They offer both popular and classical music as well as an outlet store for purchasing used CDs and more. TowerRecords.com offers a listening station of the most recent title releases. Also check out their videos and DVDs.

www.ColumbiaHouse.com

The same Columbia House membership you've seen in *TV Guide* or other magazine ads is now online. Similar membership deals are offered at its Web site: Receive twelve CDs free now and promise to buy the agreed amount in the future at club prices. Video and DVD memberships are available too.

www.Reel.com

You'll find everything you need to know about movies at Reel.com, an entertainment information site. Detailed reviews (using a four-star rating system) of what is currently playing can be found by clicking on In Theaters. Check out the reviews of Coming Attractions. An extensive alphabetical Review Archive can be browsed. Click on Shop and you can fill your cart with videos or DVDs. Check to see what's on sale or what the Studio Specials may be. In the Rental Guide section, you will find a calendar with upcoming release dates for videos as well as reviews of available videos.

www.JWPepper.com

One of the world's largest sheet music retailers has brought their catalog online. Click on Online Catalog and you'll see an array of choices, such as Early Childhood, Handbells, Choral Cantatas, and more. Click on Early Childhood and you find subheadings for Infant,

Children's Folk Music, Children's Music, and Children's Television. You can browse, or do a search by song title or by composer/artist. You can register for their newsletter, which will keep you up to date on new developments. It's as simple as giving them your e-mail address.

www.BestBuy.com

The megastore with the big yellow ticket as its logo is online and ready to help you. With BestBuy.com you can buy music and movies, and even something to play them on. Click on Movies and you can search their inventory by title or by an actor's name. If you click on Music, you can search by artist, by album, or by an individual song. BestBuy.com has a shopping assistant to help you make a decision in the electronics department. Click from a list of items, say Televisions, and answer a few questions as to what you might be looking for. Click Find It and a list of televisions, sorted by brand or price, comes up for your review. All you have to do is decide which one you want to buy.

www.CCVideo.com

Critics Choice Videos started as a specialty print catalog in the late 1980s. Their quality video selections and customer service are now available online. Their inventory lists over fifty thousand films, both current videos and more obscure titles that you might not find anywhere else. Register your e-mail address with them for exclusives and special offers.

www.Half.com

When you shop at Half.com, it's like shopping for music or videos anywhere else on the Web, except that everything here is previously owned. They have a search engine or you can browse by category. When you find what you want, you can go to a detail page for further information. Click Buy to put it in your cart. Click Checkout to complete your purchase. The difference is you're not buying the items from a company but from other Half.com members. When you find an item you want, you get to choose which copy to buy from whom, if more than one member has what you're looking for. It's not an auction house. There is no bidding. These items are used videos, CDs, and books with discounted prices listed, ready for purchase.

www.OnlyOlivia.com

Visit the Web site of the International Olivia Newton John Fan Club. You'll find her collection of CDs available for purchase, as well as a biography and interesting facts regarding her life and career. Check out the archive of photographs, dating back to her early days before stardom.

www.Margaritaville.com

The official site for Jimmy Buffett's Margaritaville, where baby boomers can purchase his CDs, cassette tapes, merchandise, even Christmas cards and stockings for the Parrothead in everyone. (Parrotheads are adult Jimmy Buffett fans; Parakeets are children.) This cross-generation entertainer has produced twenty-seven CDs of Caribbean rock and roll music. *The Parakeet Album* features songs by Jimmy Buffett sung by children for children. He has even written children's books with his daughter Savannah Jane. You can buy both albums and books here.

I loved listening to the King Family in the early sixties. Do you remember them? There were the King Sisters, the King Cousins, and at Christmas when the family got together, there were more of them than Osmonds. I lost my copy of the King Family Christmas album some-where during a move long ago. I sought out every antique store and thrift shop for years hoping for a copy. Nothing. Then as easily as one-two-three, I typed King Family into the search box on eBay.com and found two parties willing to sell their King Family Christmas albums. The first time I played my album from eBay.com, it brought goose bumps and great memories.

Sporting Goods

For those of you staying active in sports, I commend you. The Internet provides a virtual world for sport enthusiasts In any type of sport imaginable. You can learn from the pros, find places to play, and more. Since this is the shopping chapter, I'll concentrate here on Web sites where you can buy—not only for yourself but also for your grandchildren—supplies and/or gift items for a range of activities.

www.Rawlings.com

Rawlings Sporting Goods manufactures competitive sports equipment and apparel for baseball, basketball, hockey, softball, and football, as well as licensed MLB, NHL, and NCAA retail products. Click on Products or Online Store and find a terrific assortment of equipment and clothing. For the new grandchild in your family, order a personalized Rawlings seventeen-inch mini bat with the baby's name, date of birth, and measurements, or any message you want to send. Rawlings.com even offers free e-mail accounts with addresses like @home-runpower.com or @throwenheat.com.

www.FogDog.com

This seems to be an athlete's toy store. The homepage lists sports from Adventure Travel to Waterskiing; click on any listing to find equipment and apparel appropriate for that activity. Check out Departments if you're just looking for a more general scope of, say, footwear or sport watches. Click on Her.FogDog and find women's selections. Click on Outlet for bargains, super deals, and closeouts.

www.WilsonSports.com

Wilson Sporting Goods Company is one of the world's leading manufacturers of sports equipment. Focusing on making technologically advanced products that help the average player play better, their site gives you separate sport categories to click including Basketball, Baseball, Youth Sports, or Uniforms. This is an informational site only. To purchase any of their products, type in your zip code and they will give you the name and location of the nearest authorized Wilson dealer.

www.PhysicalSuccess.com

Influenced by Hollywood actors and stunt fight choreographers, this is a site built around exercise. They believe the only antiaging formula is an ongoing physical exercise commitment to yourself. It doesn't matter what sort of physical exercise routine one has as long as it's practiced at least three times each week. PhysicalSuccess.com will give you the information and a variety of products to help you enjoy exercising. Click on Kids Corner and find easy-to-use products for your grandchildren, or use them yourself to improve hand-eye coordination.

www.lpga.com
Welcome to the official Web site of the Ladies Professional Golf Association. The year 2000 was their fiftieth anniversary. Click on Teaching & Club Pro to learn from the pros. You can watch an online animated instruction of golfing tips. Click on LPGA Pro Shop and find a golfer's shopping dream presented by the *Women's Golf* catalog.

www.e-Rackets.com
The Global Racket Sports Store has been serving the public for the last thirty years and is now online. Find name brands in tennis, racquetball, and badminton rackets. Junior tennis as well as paddle tennis rackets are available. Click on Accessories and find gloves, balls, and gift items for any active racket user.

www.BassPro.com
In 1974, Bass Pro Shops published their first catalog specializing in bass fishing and outdoor products. Today at BassPro.com, you can find extensive resources and supplies for any kind of fishing and much more. Click on a

variety of categories, such as Camping & Auto, Apparel, or Footwear, and find what you need. Click on Fishing and you'll have an array of sections to choose from, including rods, reels, and tackle. You can purchase books and videos on fishing and the outdoors. Some states will now let you purchase your fishing license online at this site, but the site also provides an 800 number so you can order by phone.

FREE STUFF

Free—doesn't that get your attention? You don't have to spend a lot of money or any money on the Internet. Some companies offer free software or products for only the cost of shipping and handling. Do you love to try samples of products? How about earning prize points for trying a product sample? Go to a search engine, type in freebies or free stuff, and you can surf the Web for these budget-friendly nuggets.

www.TheFreeSite.com

Check the different categories for fresh listings and reviews of all the best freebies that are available on the Net in one convenient site. Click on Family Freebies or Free Samples and see what's new. Register for their free weekly newsletter. TheFreeSite.com is a spam-free service, so your e-mail address will not be sold to others.

www.Free2Try.com

Free2Try.com is another great site to look around. They offer hundreds of free and trial offers, conveniently organized into product categories. This site allows you to try out new products and services at little or no cost to yourself, though some companies may charge shipping and handling fees. Subscribe to the *Free2Try Dispatch* and they will send a weekly e-mail informing you of new offers.

www.1001freegifts.com

A bright, colorful site, 1001FreeGift.com has a directory of categories to choose from. Or check out Steven's Top 9 Featured Freebies. Easy to use, this site will provide you with a variety of entertainment and fun. Click on New Freebies to see their latest finds.

www.TheFreeMall.net

Here you'll find games and contests along with a list of categories to free items you can select. From Pets to Kids/Babies, find offers of all kinds. There's even a Miscellaneous Freebies section. The offers change, so check back often.

www.StartSampling.com

Register online for free samples mailed directly to you. Select one of the listed products with a green dot next to it, and it will be mailed to you free. Provide your important feedback comments to the manufacturers regarding their product. You can select a new item every twenty-four hours, and the list of products changes each month.

From apparel to zebra-striped sheets, this chapter barely scratched the surface of what is available in the virtual stores of the Internet. The convenience and choices available have made me a veteran shopper on the Internet. Enjoy your shopping adventures and let me know about your great bargains.

Do you know what the ingredients of milk toast are? Neither do I. Have you noticed split pea soup to a ten-year-old is just one step away from the green slime used on the Nickelodeon television game shows? Split pea soup and milk toast—these were the dining delicacies I could expect during childhood visits to my grandma in Northern California. Oyster stew was another strange concoction I remember being served, though I doubt a spoonful of the milky substance ever crossed my lips. A trip to visit Grammy equaled a few days of fasting for me—not a pleasant experience for a child in the epicurean department.

It's quite a different story for grandchildren today. My grandsons want Happy Meals and Kids Club Value meals when they visit my house. There's always some kind of a toy inside the colorfully printed paper bag that bribes them to eat the mass-produced cheeseburger or pressed chicken pieces. It is not considered food if it doesn't come with a plastic toy to entertain and distract.

Do the little guys care that I can cook a hot nutritious meal? Did their mom? Growing up she only wanted Kraft Macaroni and Cheese from the big blue box. I wonder why they didn't put a toy in the box as Cracker Jacks or sugared breakfast cereals did? My culinary talents were wasted over the years. Yet I can still make a mean meat loaf.

The kitchen is a great place for creating memories with the grandchildren. Use the power of the Internet for finding new culinary delights to share with them. Check out a recipe site together and choose a favorite lunch or dinner item. Make an adventurous treasure hunt to your local grocery store for the supplies you'll need and let them help as much as their ages allow. Let them use their imagination with the ingredients.

Check out the Net for many of your favorite food manufacturing companies. You will find wonderful sections of recipes, cooking tips, and ideas for holiday foods. If you don't see their Web site on the product package, do a search by typing in the name of the company and click on the search button. You'll be amazed what you'll find.

Food and Nutrition for Kids

You can use the computer to have kid-friendly menus ready and available any time for the grandchildren's visits. Mini pancakes, corn dogs, and peanut butter and jelly sandwiches are great standbys, but what about teaching our grandchildren to feel comfortable as well as creative in the kitchen? What about making incredible, culinary memories with Nana?

Keep your camera close by and capture the gastronomic moments shared with your grandchildren. These are priceless. Just try not to let them get flour all over the camera.

www.Kraft.com

Find yourself in the good hands of Kraft Foods. Their homepage offers simple, direct choices of Food and Family Recipes with Tips and Techniques. You can point and click for choices for a kid-friendly meal, and Kraft.com will help with a shopping list of ingredients you can print out. Let the little ones hold the list and the older ones can find the items. Your little sprouts will only eat breaded chicken pieces? Let them help you make a delicious dipping sauce for their chicken with Kraft's recipe using honey and Miracle Whip. They can measure and stir the ingredients, and you become the queen of the kitchen to preschoolers.

www.Dole5aDay.com

Want to play and learn about food nutrition at the same time? This site by the Dole Food Company emphasizes five servings a day of fruits and vegetables for a healthy child. It has games, recipes, and more to choose from. Meet Lucy Lettuce, for example. Did you know that lettuce is a member of the sunflower family? Neither did I. Dole also offers five songs to go along with the concept of "five a day." You can print out the lyrics to the songs. Then point and click on the sound file of each song and you and the children can sing along.

www.KidsCookingCorner.com

Two young girls have created a place where you can go to get fun recipes for children, complete with jokes and links to other enjoyable places on the Internet. This award-winning site is fun as well as informational. Click on Archives to see past recipes. There's even a recipe to make your own chicken nuggets. Check back often for new ideas and cooking tips. Be sure to leave Hillary and Ali an e-mail if you have any recipes or jokes your grandchildren would like to share with them.

www.Kelloggs.com

Those breakfast cereal people of Battle Creek, Michigan, have put together a Web site of games, nutrition information, and recipe ideas. Learn more about Tony the Tiger, and how in 1952 a close race brought him to the front of the cereal box. The Recipes section is broken out by categories and product types, you can choose or cruise. Click on Games, and your grandchildren will be entertained with puzzles and skills designed with their favorite Kellogg characters, such as Toucan Sam, in mind. Join the Kellogg Kitchen's Recipe Club for recipes e-mailed directly to you.

www.Goosie.com

Goosie's Once Upon A Recipe is a site for both young and old. Click on the egg marked Young Chefs, and Goosie will introduce children's recipes, tales, and fun games to play. Each story under Tales & Fare brings a recipe with it. The site creators take classic fairy tales and folklore and give them a humorous, culinary twist while encouraging nutritious, fun-filled activities, reading and math skills, even self-esteem. Read Peter Cottontail's story with your grandchildren and find that it ends with a recipe for Mrs. Rabbit's Hoppin' Good Stuffed Cabbage. You can even purchase online a copy of the book *Once Upon A Recipe*, which your grandchildren can take home with them.

www.IloveCheese.com

From the American Dairy Association comes everything you ever wanted to know about cheese. Click on All about Cheese and you will see the Meltability section, which gives tips on heating and melting cheese. Recipe categories include Lunch and Brunch, Finger Foods, and Family Favorite Entrees. See which flavor is featured in the latest Cheese Spotlight and learn its history and receive some fabulous recipes. Did you know mozzarella is packed in water for freshness? Did you know I'm older than provolone? Sign up to receive *Cheese Bytes*, the official, information-packed, online cheese newsletter of the American Dairy Association at your e-mail address.

www.Cyberspaceag.com

Click on the picture of a cyber farm somewhere in Kansas to begin your nutritious adventure. Tina Tractor will be your tour guide through the menu of items under Star Guide. Click on Cosmic Crops and find your space base for exploring plants that farmers grow in Kansas. Visit Planet Wheat, catch a Soybean Star, circle the Sunflower Sun, or chase the Corn Comet. Or choose the Cosmic Café for out-of-this-world recipes. Women Involved in Farm Economics (WIFE), a national agriculture organization, sponsors CyberSpace Farm. Log on to Kansas WIFE and check out who they are and what they do to promote agriculture.

www.got-milk.com

Warning: This site moos at you when it first opens. That's how fresh it is. Kids in the Kitchen is a good place to start moo-ving around. You learn to make a glass of milk more fun by stirring in food coloring, such as a drop of yellow to make Yellow Moon Milk or a drop of blue for Blue Jungle Juice. Click on Better Bones for healthy advice and information on calcium, something even grandmothers need to remember. Got-milk.com offers trivia, games, and contests for the grandchildren, so check back often. Want to see the famous milk mustache ads? Go to www.whymilk.com.

www.doughboy.com

Tickling the Pillsbury Doughboy's tummy is something the grandkids will love. Passing your cursor over his picture makes him giggle. Click to enter this delightful site for fun and information about the Pillsbury Doughboy. Click on Doughboy Kitchen to find recipes using Pillsbury products that will bring a smile to the grandkids at the dining table. Let them help by wrapping a hot dog in a crescent roll or unrolling pizza crust dough to make stuffed-crust pizza. While they're eating their delicious creations, check out the Doughboy Merchandise for Pillsbury's entire catalog of items online. And after the kids are done eating, let them play the Catch-A-Cookie game under Doughboy Games.

www.Mcdonalds.com

Yes, even the Golden Arches are online. Click on Ronald and Friends to let your little ones enjoy their favorite characters. By clicking on the different scenes, you will go deeper into Ronald McDonaldland and find games to play. Grimace has a match-the-squares game, and he'll let you know how many tries it took to solve the puzzle. Don't forget to click on Big Book of Fun for games and puzzles you can print out.

www.KidsCandy.org

Did you know a one-and-a-quarter-ounce piece of milk chocolate contains about the same amount of caffeine as a cup of decaffeinated coffee. An average of six milligrams of caffeine can be found in both an ounce of milk chocolate and a cup of decaf, while a cup of regular coffee contains between 65 and 150 milligrams of caffeine. Not only does KidsCandy.org provide you with mouth-watering recipes for sweets, but you can also click on Health & Nutrition for helpful information. Click on Brain Candy for more fun facts and trivia.

www.scoreone.com/kids_kitchen

Kids Kitchen is a colorful site of recipes submitted by children of all ages. Click on Major Messes for recipes that "make the most mess but taste the best" according to the young cooks. Click on Sweet and Sticky for yummy treats that can be made up in minutes. Let your grandchildren submit a favorite recipe, and maybe it will be chosen as Creation of the Month, which means kids voted it the number one recipe.

www.FoodForTots.com

Dr. Janice Woolley and Jennifer Pugmire have created a Web site for the discriminating palate of toddlers and preschoolers. Click on Recipes and Tips for selections of snacks and beverages as well as meals. FoodForTots.com is based on Woolley and Pugmire's book *Food for Tots*, and all recipes have been kid tested. You'll find a great recipe for playing dough too.

Cooking something scrumptious and nutritious for a child is more fun than just taking something out of a paper bag from a fast-food restaurant. Some kids, however, won't believe that it will be more fun for them. They'll need some convincing. Don't just wait until the holidays to make them special treats. Plan a tea party or a sandwich party, and use the Internet to help show them the fun in preparation and cooking as well as the fun of enjoying the finished product.

Cooking and Food for Grandma

The Net offers you sites featuring your favorite television chefs, information on culinary schools around the world, cookbooks, recipes, cookware, accessories, and much, much more. No longer do you need to worry about what to make for a special holiday occasion at the home of your adult children or how to spice up a Sunday dinner in the middle of winter. Feeling adventurous for something tasty that you've never tried before? You'll find it on the Internet. Get out your best apron and enjoy the sites ahead of you.

www.LightLiving.com

Winner of a variety of Web site awards, Light-Living.com offers you recipes and information for making healthy choices in your eating. Nutritional information will not be found at the bottom of the recipes because you are given choices as to the ingredients you want to use. (There are differences in light margarines, for example.) Enjoy the tasty nutritious recipes listed each week, or click on Recipe Archives and search through past listings. Click on Forum to check out the LightLiving.com message board.

www.CookingWithPatty.com

Want authentic Italian recipes? CookingWithPatty.com is the right place. The recipes here are direct from Verona, Italy. Patty lives in the northeastern area of Italy so her recipes are based on northern Italian food. Many of us in the United States think of Italian food as dishes found in the southern region of Italy. You can check out the Top Ten recipe list based on visitors to the site, or click on Recipes for easy-to-choose categories such as Pasta or Gnocchi. Seasonal menu ideas are available or check out a menu for a specific holiday. Patty adds a new recipe to her site each week. Sign up for her newsletter and she'll let you know when she changes her recipes.

www.Eat.com

With a name like Eat.com, it has to be Italian—and it is. Welcome to Mama's Cucina! The people from Lipton, Inc. bring you ideas using Ragú sauces and Pizza Quick. Click on Recipes to see a list of choices such as pasta, chicken, and cheese creations. Mouth-watering temptations such as No Boil Baked Ziti, or Hearty Lasagna Rolls are just a sample of what you'll find. You can learn a little Italian while you're checking out the recipes. Click on A Happy Family and find out how to say "Clean your room or no spaghetti for you tonight" along with half a dozen other phrases. Mama thinks of everything to keep you satisfied and busy on this site.

www.BettyCrocker.com

The name we know and love is online to help you with kitchen and cooking concerns. The homepage sets you up with a warm feeling with choices like What's for Dinner and What's on Hand. When your kitchen supplies are low, enjoy using What's on Hand to find out what you could make for dinner. Type in the ingredients you have on hand, and BettyCrocker.com will come up with a list of recipe solutions. Click on Recipes for a journey into the quality of online Betty Crocker cookbooks. Choose by food category, or do a search with a keyword. Click Online Bakery and you can order gourmet cookies and brownies straight from the Betty Crocker ovens. They're made from scratch according to special recipes and are packed with the finest ingredients. They're a perfect way to send a sweet greeting to your friends and family.

www.Cooking.com

Visit Cooking.com for a one-stop kitchen site. It offers an assortment of cookware, accessories, and specialty foods. Click Tableware & Glassware under Departments to find an assortment of everything you need in place settings and more. A huge selection of recipes in a variety of cuisines is available. Get expert cooking tips and check the cooking glossary. Shop for cookware, cutlery, utensils, and more in the Gift Center. This site is for people who love to dish up something with love.

www.AmericanSpice.com

Whether you're looking for the unique taste of ginger from Asia or red-hot salsa from Texas, AmericanSpice.com has it. The Great American Spice Company offers a complete line of exquisite spices and blends prepared in small batches to guarantee freshness. Their spice blends are reported to be carefully prepared from authentic family recipes unique to ethnic groups or geographic areas of the world. Amish, Bayou, and Cajun are just the beginning of their extensive inventory spice blends. Click on Browse

Our Recipes for choices from appetizers to side dishes. The Vegetarian Section guarantees that none of the products contain meat or meat by-products.

www.Wine.com

Everything you ever wanted to know about wine but were afraid to ask can be found here. You can buy wine here too. Wine.com gives you in-depth information about the wines being offered and the people who made them. Distressed by the trend in the wine industry to reduce wine marketing to a numerical scoring system for ribbons, Wine.com feels this can be particularly harmful to the small artisan winemakers. You can order online for yourself and for holidays and gift giving. They feature wines from the best vintners, so you can count on getting a quality bottle every time.

www.WineWatchGuide.com

Each year judges evaluate thousands of wines entered in eleven major U.S. competitions. Some of these wines delight the judges one competition after another. Knowing which wines are winners can save you time and expense in finding your favorites. This site is devoted to the best of those award-winning wines. Wines are sorted not only by type but also by number of prizes won. Bargain hunters can find wines that have won the most awards and sell for the lowest price.

www.StarChefs.com

Want to know what the big cooks are making in their kitchens? Click on Chefs from the homepage and see an alphabetical listing of the top names in culinary arts. Each choice will give you a brief biography including when and how the chef started in the culinary field and a recent interview with the master chef. Click on Recipes to see a list of dishes picked specifically by that chef. Cookbook authors are also listed with a sample recipe. StarChefs.com has evolved into a megasite of restaurant e-commerce and ideas as well as spotlighting the people behind the aprons.

www.FoodTV.com

The Food Network is online for your convenience and entertainment. Click on one of your favorite shows, *Food 911*, *Essence of Emeril*, and *The Naked Chef* to find their latest recipes and show information. Terms, Tips and Ingredients from the homepage is an excellent resource. Type in a word from a cookbook or recipe and it will give you the definition. There's a fat and calorie counter. What about ingredient substitutions? Type in your missing ingredient, and they'll give you a list of products that will work in a pinch. Click on Wine for Food to find a list of appropriate vintages to pour with your main course.

Recipes

We all have our favorite secret recipes, passed down from family or friends, stashed somewhere in a cupboard or drawer. Slips of paper and index cards with treasured ingredients produce wonderful, tantalizing delights when you're done. What if you had the world's largest cookbook and recipe collection at your fingertips? For times when you just want to peruse recipes for yourself and family, when a bookshelf of worn recipe books, with pages dog-eared and splattered, won't do, you'll find the Net becomes a virtual kitchen of imagination.

www.AllRecipes.com

A virtual cookbook at your fingertips, you can find almost anything with just a click. Allrecipes.com currently consists of twenty chapters from Appetizer recipes to Christmas recipes; Main Dish recipes to Soup; Thanksgiving to Vegetarian recipes. Click on Shop and visit a culinary store of utensils and dinnerware. You can set up your own recipe box on their site. MyRecipe Box is a free, private, personalized, and easy-to-use meal planning resource that allows you to store, organize, and share your favorite recipes with other users on the Allrecipes.com site. They have also entered into an alliance with *Diabetes Forecast*, the healthy living magazine of the American Diabetes Association (ADA). Allrecipes.com now provides a selection of diabetic recipes from the ADA.

www.GoodHousekeeping.com

Click on Eat Well/Stay Healthy on the homepage of this famous magazine. Use their Recipe Finder as a search vehicle for what you need. You can click on the type of dish you're looking for and/or the main ingredients. Maybe you're looking for a specific cuisine? Just click on your choices and click Search. It's that fast and simple. The Good Housekeeping Institute brings recipes and tips right to your computer.

www.NabiscoRecipes.com

The famous Nabisco people have put together a Web site full of great recipes and information. Click on What's for Dinner? to find an easy-to-use list of recipes where you can scan quickly for preparation and cooking times. Under Snacking Tips, you can click on a brand logo, such as Triscuits, for serving suggestions and delicious recipes. Click on Hints for the Kitchen and find helpful tips from Heloise herself. A food encyclopedia is an additional feature.

www.my-meals.com

Make meal planning and grocery shopping easier and more enjoyable by visiting this Web site. It can also help you put great meals on your dinner table faster and save money as well. At Recipe Center you can browse through selections by courses or cuisines, or select Special Diets and find ideas for low-sodium or low-fat dishes. At Suggested Meals you will find holiday menus, weekly menus, and what to do with the leftovers. With just a few clicks, you can print detailed shopping lists based on the recipes you've selected.

Gourmet Food

Interestingly enough, on the Internet "gourmet" does not merely mean continental cuisine and food preparation. Gourmet also includes specialty diets for diabetics, heart disease, and others. A search may lead you to many interesting sites offering a variety of food suggestions—from spicy Caribbean to mild caviar to a palatable bland diet. Type the word "gourmet" at your favorite search engine and find out what kind of new adventures await you. Tantalize your taste buds with different recipes and flavors. Order gourmet sauces or coffees to be delivered right to your door. You'll be amazed what you can find on the Web.

www.Epicurious.com

A great selection of basic to gourmet recipes and tips, Epicurious.com has much to offer. Choose the Kid-Friendly selection from Recipes to find such delights as cheeseburger meatloaf. Click on Restaurant Recipes or Meatless for a different flare. Switch to *Bon Appétit* or *Gourmet,* and you'll get the latest articles and information online from these tantalizing magazines.

www.globalgourmet.com

Featuring new content every weekday, you may want to visit this site often. Departments include Culinary Sleuth and Cookbook Profiles. Feature stories add information on recipes from around the world.

www.ffgc.com

The Fancy Food Gourmet Club catalog is online with a variety of products, prices, and service. Products are selected to meet four basic criteria: highest quality, distinctive or award winning, those able to be priced at a value to customers, and products that they personally enjoy and use to entertain relatives and friends. Click on Shop with Us and see selections such as Smoked Salmon, Russian and Domestic Caviar, Patés and Mousses, and more. Accessories to use with your gourmet delicacies can also be found. Shopping cart convenience is available in buying products for yourself or as gifts.

www.GourmetShoppes.com

A virtual shop galore is what you'll find here. Each category, from food and beverage to health and beauty, is a link to a list of shops carrying these products on the Internet. Gourmet Foods and Delicacies range from Asian to Seafood shops. Click on Store Directory and find the names of the shops listed by categories.

Nutritiously Gourmet offers balanced menus with recipes a cut above average for the everyday cook. If you want to eat healthy and enjoy good food at the same time, you have come to the right place. These meals are both nutritious and delicious, with a slight European flair. Click on Introduction, then About the Author to find that Jane A. Rubey, M.P.H., R.D. founded Nutritiously Gourmet, a cooking school, in 1991. All those letters after her name mean she holds a master's degree in public health: nutrition (M.P.H.) and is a registered dietitian (R.D.). A sample of her menus includes Kabocha Squash with Dried Fruit Chutney, Slow-Simmered Red Cabbage and Apples, Ginger-Scented Mashed Yams, and Broccoli Carrot Tofu Timbales.

Buying Food Online—Specialty Shops

You can order almost any food imaginable from the Internet and it will be delivered right to your door. Satisfaction for intense cravings can be had if you don't mind waiting the indicated delivery time. This isn't Pizza Hut where you can expect it hot and fresh. For most of these sites, we are talking a minimum of three to five business days for delivery. That won't work if you're in a gotta-have-it-now kind of mood.

In selected areas you can buy your groceries online. Remember the days when the iceman and the milkman delivered cold products right to the door? Now it's the grocer for our grandchildren.

Internet food shopping is a pleasant solution to gift buying and party planning. It's also fun to do just because you're special and you deserve a delicious treat.

www.Schwans.com

Here's where convenience and quality have blended into a wonderful food delivery service. A company that started out as a family dairy and moved to home delivery in 1952, Schwan's has grown to a nationally known customer service–oriented food delivery business. Check out their delicious menus. It doesn't get much easier to serve your family delicious, wholesome foods for breakfast, lunch, and dinner using Schwan's foods right from your freezer to the oven or microwave. And don't forget to order their signature ice cream, still the great recipe of nearly fifty years. Home delivery is available in all forty-eight states of the continental United States.

www.DansChocolates.com

No, you won't gain an ounce looking at the scrumptious photos of chocolate on the homepage of this site. Dans-Chocolates.com came from Dan Cunningham's concept of using the Internet to deliver the freshest, handmade chocolates available while donating a percentage of revenues to charity. Partnering with a longtime friend at Blue Mountain Arts (www.bluemountain.com from chapter 1), he created a company with charity at its heart—the cream filling, if you will. DansChocolates.com guarantees candies to be delivered within seven days of production.

www.Chocoholic.com

Chocolatiers are listed by geographic regions for you so you can find a real chocolatier in your part of the country. Your order will be shipped directly from their kitchens. Click on Recipes to find delicious treats you can make at home.

www.ShoppingPlace.com

Here you will find information on and hundreds of retail shops for chocolate and coffee. Click on Chocolate Corner and you can search for types of chocolate, or at the bottom of the page choose a selection such as Chocolate Shoppes or Chocolate History. Go over to Coffee Café and you can search by your favorite brand or browse through such sections as The Bean and Perfect Cup. At Ask the Expert, you can post your question and the owners of chocolate and coffee shops around the globe will assist ShoppingPlace.com in providing the answers.

www.GourmetCoffeeClub.com

Coffee lovers are welcomed here. Designer packages of preground, ready-to-brew coffee can be mailed directly to you. Small batch processing keeps the roasted hand-picked, grown-at-high-elevations Arabica beans fresh. Choose standard brands such as Kenya Blend or Seattle City Roast. Try one of their flavored varieties such as Southern Pecan. Are you more of a tea drinker? Click on Ashbys to find a list of mouthwatering flavors such as Cinnamon Plum and Vanilla Spice. In either coffee or tea, you can choose individual flavors or try a gourmet pack. Decaf flavors are noted. Not to be overlooked, click on Cocoa Amore for their list of delicious mixes such as Chocolate Butter Rum and Chocolate Raspberry.

www.FarAwayFoods.com

With a name like Far Away Foods, you should be able to find something for the finickiest palate. Click on Syrups and Honey to find luscious tropical syrups from Hawaiian Plantations, or Italian honeys from Rustichella d' Abruzzo. How about Outback Mustard from Australia with baby horseradish seasoning? Or mustards with wine? Click What's New to stay on top of new arrivals.

www.eCake.net

Celebrate any occasion with cake hand-delivered to home or office anywhere in the United States and Canada. ECake.net, working with The WireACake/HB Bakery Connection through its network of member bakeries, can arrange for a birthday cake, anniversary cake, or any other holiday occasion to be delivered fresh. Debora George, founder of HB Inc., created a network of bakeries that would give people a way to wire a cake to any city in the country. Choose cake size, flavorings, colors, and decorations.

www.MyGrandmas.com

Find an assortment of delicious New England–style coffee cakes available for delivery. Choose from a cinnamon walnut in regular or low-fat or a Granny Smith apple. Click Hillary's All Natural Baking Mixes. Keep a couple of these on hand for those days when your grandchildren want home-baked cookies or brownies, but you don't have the energy to make a mess in the kitchen. How can you miss with a flavor called Double Chocolate Hunks of Chunks Cookie Mix? Packages stay fresh for one year. Hillary's is certified kosher by the Orthodox Union.

www.HometownFavorites.com

Here's a fun spot to try. Ever wondered if they still make the candies and products we loved from our past? Remember the commercial "I want my Maypo?" Do they still make the hot cereal? Check out what Colleen Chapin, president of this small family-owned business, has created. You can order Fizzies Sparkling Drink Tablets. How many of you as a child tried to suck on one and ended up looking like a mad dog? Can't find what you're looking for at the online store? They have an e-mail and feedback forum. HometownFavorites.com's research team will scout for the items and get back to you on their results.

www.SouthernFood.com

Do you know the difference between Creole and Cajun foods? SouthernFood.com says Creole is city style and Cajun is rural in Louisiana. There is no single style of food in the South, and this Web site does justice to all. Check out the online shop and find something new to your taste buds. Try boiled peanuts from the Georgia Farmer's Market. Or try Gullah Gourmet's She Crab Soup Mix or a can of condensed Blue Crab Bay's Clam and Corn Chowder. Don't forget a bottle of Kentucky's Mint Julep Syrup. SouthernFood.com offers a variety of gift baskets filled with the flavors of the South. Or customize your own for that special person in your life.

www.Shop-Maine.com

You will find a selection of Maine-made products on this site. You can choose from seafoods under the Coastal Waters of Maine category or look under For the Chef of Maine for interesting items. What about a bag of Wood-Prairie Farm organically grown, gourmet potatoes, with names like Yukon Gold, All-Blue, and Rose Gold? Included are recipes and information on how to keep the potatoes fresh. Shop-Maine.com also offers Cap Morrill's fresh Maine lobsters and shellfish, steamer clams, and farm-grown, cultured mussels for overnight delivery by Fed Ex to your door. Bet you didn't know that Maine lobster is lower in fat, cholesterol, and calories than is the light meat of chicken. Neither did I.

Online Grocers

Home-delivered grocery services are proliferating on the Internet. Most companies are serving in limited areas at this time. Check if you can receive their services in your city by typing in your zip code. If not available yet, most of these companies will take your name and e-mail address to advise you as soon as their delivery trucks start coming to your region. Minimum purchase amounts may apply.

Online grocers' prices are usually competitive with those at your local markets. And just like your local stores, most will offer weekly specials and accept manufacturers' coupons. Unlike shopping at your local store, you'll be less inclined to impulse buy. In fact, you may even save money by using delivery services rather than reaching for all those additional items that are not on your grocery list.

Though your first visit to a site may take some time—it is like walking up and down the aisles of a new grocery store—most sites have a feature that records the items you've ordered in the past. This makes your subsequent shopping visits easier and faster. Remember: You can place your order any time day or night with these sites as the Internet is always open for business. Most ask for a specific date and time for delivery.

www.Peapod.com

Based out of Illinois, Peapod.com offers quality service along with name-brand products delivered right to your door. They offer delivery of fresh produce, meats, baked goods, and nonperishable items to many metropolitan areas. However, they also provide a service called Peapod Packages that delivers nonperishable groceries, household items, pet supplies, and health and beauty care products to addresses across the continental United States. Create special care packages for friends and family.

www.HomeGrocer.com

Based out of the state of Washington, HomeGrocer.com has merged with WebVan.com, another home grocery service (see below), in an attempt to provide the best quality at low prices. The white trucks with the big peach logo on the sides are delivering in more areas all the time. Each truck has three temperature settings for your groceries: ambient, refrigerated, and freezing. Don't forget to click on the Specials tab. These are changed each Wednesday.

www.WebVan.com

WebVan.com services the greater areas of Atlanta, Georgia; Chicago, Illinois; Sacramento and the San Francisco Bay Area of California. WebVan@Work will also deliver to your place of business (if in their delivery area) for meetings and office parties. Be sure to check out WebVan.com's chef-prepared meals. Using only quality ingredients, the meals have been fully cooked and then quickly chilled, so when heated at home, they emerge from the oven or microwave delicious and hot.

www.OnlineGrocer.ca

This service delivers thousands of name-brand products, fresh produce, deli, and dairy items to the Ottawa, Ontario (Canada) area.

Most national-chain supermarkets are creating Web sites to advertise their specials and services to users like you. Check out your favorite store to see if they have an address on the Internet. Ask the store manager. Ralphs.com offers online coupons and a store locator. Pavilions.com lists their weekly specials and provides ValuePlus Club membership information.

From a perfect cup of coffee to a gift basket for your son and daughter-in-law's anniversary, you'll find a delicatessen of choices on the Net. Food, the Internet, and you make a great culinary team.

Grandma Called the Doctor and the Doctor Said

I don't know about you, but one day I was flipping through a specialty catalog and saw a small cross-stitched throw pillow saying, "I'm out of estrogen, and I have a gun." I laughed till I had tears in my eyes. I can relate to that statement. Menopause is alive and well for me, and I should probably come with a warning label across my forehead.

Specific Ailments

Where did I go to find out the most recent and up-to-date information regarding menopause without having to make an appointment with my HMO? On the Internet. After another sleepless night with damp sheets, I turned the computer on and asked a search engine. I typed in the word "women," used a plus sign after it, then added night sweats. I wanted to eliminate as much as possible that might come up for men or children having night sweats. A lengthy list of Web sites came up with titles such as Libido and Night Sweats. Once I started clicking through the Web pages, I found I have most of the symptoms of perimenopause. I can't say this would work for most ailments, but it hit the nail on the head for this one. The Web sites helped me understand what was happening to my body in simple language. They gave me facts to take to my doctor when I finally got in to see him. Did I want to ask for estrogen replacement, what were the pros and cons of that decision? Yes, I take my little green pill every day. Like that little throw pillow says, you wouldn't want to see me out of estrogen. It's not pretty.

You can look up specific illnesses at a search engine. See if there are Web sites maintained by major foundations and nonprofits that do research, advocacy, and/or education on particular ailments or conditions. You'll be amazed at the amount of information and support available. Here are some samples:

www.Cancer.org

The American Cancer Society has put together an informative and easy-to-use site. At the Cancer Resource Center Overview, there is a drop-down menu of cancer types. Information is also available in Spanish. Click on Living with Cancer and find answers to questions that address the day-to-day concerns of a person living with cancer or their family members. Here are some of the questions they address: How do I know I am reacting normally or if I am depressed? Can my attitude influence the course of my cancer? What are the newest cancer treatments? What kinds of American Cancer Society programs would help me cope with my illness? An easy-to-use Glossary is also available for understanding cancer terms.

www.AmericanHeart.org

The official Web site of the American Heart Association has much to offer. Click on their Heart and Stroke A-Z Guide for easy-to-use references. Find out about the American Stroke Association and the warning signs of a stroke. Click on Risk Awareness and learn more about the warning signs of a heart attack. Or check out Children And Heart Disease and gain knowledge about the normal heart of a child and how it works, or about heart murmurs. Resources And Information provide links to other Web sites for the heart. Dietary guidelines for a healthy heart are available from this site.

www.Diabetes.org

The mission of the American Diabetes Association (ADA) is to prevent and cure diabetes, and to improve the lives of all people affected by this disease. Read diabetes-related stories and official ADA news releases in the News from ADA section. If you or someone you love is newly diagnosed with diabetes, you can click on the Newly Diagnosed section for a wealth of medical treatment and nutritional information. Visit the ADA bookstore to order such books as *Guide to Raising a Child with Diabetes*, *Women and Diabetes*, or a variety of cookbooks.

www.Arthritis.org

The goals of the Arthritis Foundation are to help prevent and find the cure for arthritis as well as to improve the quality of life for those affected by arthritis. The menu on the left of the Web site gives you three main choices: Information, Action, and Tools. Click on Starting Points to find the statement that fits your concerns, such as "I've just been told I have arthritis" or "I've had arthritis for years." Click on the applicable statement to learn more. Or skip right to Arthritis Answers, the place for information regarding the disease and treatments. Message boards are a place to ask questions and discuss concerns with others—both people afflicted with arthritis and/or their family members.

www.MichaelJFox.org

Michael J. Fox, a prominent actor, left the successful television situation comedy *Spin City* in the spring of 2000. At that time, he announced that he has Parkinson's disease and would be focusing his energies on the work of his new foundation. The Michael J. Fox Foundation for Parkinson's Research was born out of Michael's determination to raise new monies needed to fund the research for a cure for Parkinson's. The foundation is working with the Parkinson's Action Network (PAN), which seeks to raise national awareness of Parkinson's disease and the need for government support of Parkinson's research.

Click on Links & Resources to find links to the Parkinson's Institute and National Institute of Neurological Disorders and Strokes. Click on Glossary for an extended list of medical terms and definitions.

www.nmss.org

Welcome to the National Multiple Sclerosis Society Web site. People coping with multiple sclerosis, as well as friends and family of those with MS, can find information, resources, and support in dealing with the varied symptoms associated with this lifelong neurological disorder. Click on MS Information and find an easy-to-use listing for your specific concerns, such as What Causes MS, Symptoms, or For the Newly Diagnosed. Information is available in Spanish as well as other languages such as French, Portuguese, Italian, and more.

www.mdausa.org

At the Web site of Muscular Dystrophy Association (MDA), you will find news and information about neuromuscular diseases, MDA research, and services for adults and children with neuromuscular diseases as well as their families. Click on Ask The Experts. See listings of questions and concerns by people like you looking for current research developments and medical management of these conditions. Post a question of your own. Clinics/Services will tell you the closest available hospital-affiliated clinic when you type in your zip code. Check out Community Programs, or watch a clip from the latest Jerry Lewis MDA telethon. Information is also available in Spanish.

www.Menopause-Online.com

The latest headlines from medicine, science, and pharmacology regarding menopause are presented in nonscientific, nonmedical language. Alternative treatments are touted here, with herbal and nutritional answers to some of the common physical and emotional complaints of menopause. Take an online test to see if hormones are for you. HRT (hormone replacement therapy) comes with good news and bad news. It may increase the risk of breast and endometrial cancer while definitely decreasing the risk of heart disease and bone fractures resulting from osteoporosis. Check out their message boards to see what other women are saying about menopause.

www.PreventBlindness.org

Prevent Blindness America is a national volunteer eye health and safety organization dedicated to fighting blindness and saving sight. Now online, you can print out eye charts and take an informal eye examination in your own home. Take the Near Vision Test for Adults or the Age-Related Macular Degeneration Test using an Amsler Grid. Macular Degeneration is a disorder at the back of the eye in which the central part of one's vision is blocked as if a blurred area had been placed in the center of the picture. How to do eye tests for children using the E chart and a pointing game is also explained.

www.Alzheimers.org

At the Alzheimer's Disease Education and Referral (ADEAR) Center's Web site, you will find information about Alzheimer's disease and related disorders. Alzheimer's is one of the most common causes of the loss of mental function also known as dementia. ADEAR Center is a service of the National Institute on Aging (NIA). Click on What's New Here, and find a list of the latest articles, or click on NIA News for releases and information on Alzheimer's.

I took care of my mother during her last year and the living room became her studio apartment set up with a hospital bed and other medical conveniences. As a caregiver of an aging parent, I was to enter a new world of using antiseptics, caring for bedsores, and learning to give injections.

As her physical symptoms became severe, I found support and what I needed to know about chronic obstructive pulmonary disease and congestive heart failure out on the information superhighway. I was ready for any change in her condition, from swollen feet to side effects from her medications. She was my best friend, and the Web sites helped me fight her medical battles for her and make sure she was as comfortable as humanly possible under these difficult circumstances.

Children's Health

My first year as a grandmother began in June of 1994. It was, of course, the same important year for my daughter as well—her first year as a mom. We now shared the invisible thread of motherhood. Though many of the responsibilities of a mother and a grandmother differ, one responsibility we will always share is caring for our children and keeping them safe, healthy, and happy. We went to the Internet to discover the latest in child nutrition, development, and health.

Ways of caring for children change with each generation. My mother was there to provide her methods of child rearing based on a mixture of common sense and keeping your fingers crossed. Great-grandmothers are treasures. My last memories of baby formula were back in the Nixon administration, and I used a concoction mixed with brewer's yeast and Vitamin E drops, a la Adelle Davis theory.

Remember: Information on these sites is of a general nature. Actual diagnosis and treatment by a licensed pediatrician is essential in the case of illness or injury.

www.KidsDoctor.com

This site (maintained by Dr. Lewis Coffin, a pediatrician in Georgia) provides quick, simple information on kid-related health topics. Begin by typing in a keyword, such as "pacifier," in the search box. You'll get a list of easy-to-read articles on the topic. Click on Q&A (Questions and Answers) to learn what others are asking about regarding children as well as the answers to their questions.

www.BabyCenter.com

BabyCenter.com divides its site into the sections of Pre-conception, Pregnancy, Baby, and Toddler. Or click on Topics A-Z for quick information on a certain topic. Check out Ask the Experts. Babycenter.com offers information, products, and will send e-mail newsletters geared to different ages—from newborn to twelve months or the toddler stages of thirteen to thirty-six months. Special features include a pregnancy calendar and baby namer.

www.KidSource.com

Created by parents seeking to share in-depth information on education and health care, KidSource Online works to give parents and caregivers greater resources and advice. Select Newborn, Toddler, Preschool, or K-12 for What's New in articles regarding a specific age with information on education, health, development, and safety issues. The variety and quality of the information is excellent. Check out the Online Forums. The forums are for parents and educators to meet, to share advice, and to talk about the children in their lives. Do a search for a topic in the forum section, or click on something from the list provided. Books, videos, and software are for sale in the online Shop.

www.PreemieStore.com

Whether you have a five-pound preemie or a brand-new little person under two pounds, PreemieStore.com has specialty goodies to comfort you and delight your family. More than just products for the littlest arrivals into the world, the site includes articles, growth charts, and more. Click on Weight Chart and find an easy-to-use Gram Weight conversion chart, which is ready to print out. Every item in the catalog serves a purpose: to comfort a baby, promote its growth and development, and inform and support families to enjoy and be proud of their tiny newborns.

www.KidsDentalCare.com

Dr. Michael Buccino, a pediatric dentist, and his staff have created this Web site not only to promote their office and services but also to give the public an easy source of answers and information concerning a child's dental needs. Click on FAQ (Frequently Asked Questions) and find out answers to general questions on children's dental care: At what age should a child start visiting a dentist? What can you do about the pain of teething? Should a cavity in a baby tooth be filled? Click on What Every Parent Should Know and get informative articles about what to expect during a first visit to the dentist, and more.

www.KidsDentistry.com

Dr. Homer Sedighi and staff have put together a comprehensive look at how and which teeth children will lose as they are growing up. The graphics in understanding baby teeth versus permanent teeth from age six to age eighteen are extremely informative.

www.aapd.org

The American Academy of Pediatric Dentistry (AAPD) is online to promote its dedication to improving and maintaining the oral health of infants, children, adolescents, and people with special health-care needs. Click on Parent Information to find the latest information from the AAPD. Learn about Children, Water, and Fluoride. Check out Thumb, Finger and Pacifier Habits. Then let the grandchildren click on No Adults! to enjoy Cyberkids, games, and fun.

www.add.org

Is your school-age grandchild afflicted with Attention Deficit Disorder, or ADD? What used to be classified as orneriness or extra exuberance in a young student is today more likely to be labeled ADD by professionals. The National Attention Deficit Disorder Association wants you to know the facts. Read the latest medical and legal articles and issues surrounding ADD. Check out the message centers and community boards where you can hear from other parents and grandparents who have gone through the testing for ADD and/or the side effects of certain medications. What is the difference between ADD and adolescent or middle school attitude, and how can you tell? Find the support you need to help your grandchildren be better, stronger individuals by visiting this site.

www.vh.org

Click on Children's Virtual Hospital to find answers, information, and support for children having to go to a hospital. The people at Children's Hospital of Iowa and the University of Iowa Health Care have put together this tremendous site. Click on Common Problems for an alphabetical list of concerns from acne to well-child care. Click on For Kids and find additional links to other medical Web sites.

www.Puberty101.com

Where was this site when we were growing up? Puberty101.com was founded by Mr. J. Geoff Malta, adolescent therapist, as a place for teens to ask questions and get honest, open answers about puberty. This site is not recommended for anyone under the age of thirteen without parental guidance. Sections are separated into Guys, Girls, and a Guys and Girls general discussion. The sensitive topics are explicit yet tastefully handled. Drawings are available to illustrate certain adolescent developments in the body. Puberty101.com offers information into the chaotic world of today's youth and their responses to the changes in their bodies.

As an infant, my grandson Isaiah developed a high fever one weekend. His ears didn't seem sore, and he didn't have a runny nose. He'd had a physical and inoculations three days earlier, but that couldn't be the problem, could it? Usually an infant reacts to his shots in the first twenty-four hours, not days later. The doctor had given my daughter a flyer on a new vaccine Isaiah had gotten, and we looked it up on the Internet. The Web site stated that three to five days after receiving the vaccine a child could develop a spiked fever.

Instead of a miserable two-hour adventure at the emergency room, we gave Isaiah a cool bath and some Tylenol drops, and monitored his fever. The fever broke, as suddenly as it had appeared. My daughter reported the situation to the pediatrician's office by phone the next day, and they said we did everything they would have recommended.

Comprehensive Health Information

Most larger health sites have a variety of information sections to them. You find the latest news and articles, an ask-the-expert section, and message boards or forums to ask other users about their experiences, and more.

Let me state that the advertising you will find on these sites is in part what funds the "free" Internet information concept; the site sponsor does not necessarily endorse what is being advertised. Look to be sure the site conforms to the HON (Health on the Net Foundation) code of ethics for health-care sites.

www.DiscoveryHealth.com

From the same quality people of Discovery Communications, the cable programmer, comes Discovery Health Media, a comprehensive medical information site. Here you can do a search on a keyword such as "measles," or click on the convenient category Diseases and Conditions and be able to look things up alphabetically. Click on Healthy Tools for interesting facts and trivia. Check out Expert Opinion where health professionals share answers to their patients' most common questions.

www.MayoHealth.org

The Mayo Clinic Health Oasis is a source of reliable health information from the well-known Mayo Clinic. A team of Mayo physicians, scientists, writers, and educators directs this site. MayoHealth.com is updated each weekday to bring you the most relevant health information. You can do a search or click on one of their centers, such as Arthritis, Children's, Nutrition, or Women's. Each center will give you headline topics and a list of general information subjects. Click on Headline Watch for current events in the world of medical information. Check out the archive of medical reports.

www.WebMD.com

WebMD.com facilitates information exchange among consumers, physicians, and health-care institutions. You begin by clicking on Consumer on the homepage. Now you have a range of easy-to-use choices. On the left are headings such as Health and Wellness, Medical Info (which gives more general information in the areas of self-care), and Drugs and Herbs. In the center of the page you can click on specific areas, such as Newly Diagnosed, Start Here, and choose the relevant topic from the menu. Talk with People Who Understand is where you can post a message and get feedback from people with the same concerns as you.

www.CBSHealthWatch.com

CBSHealthWatch offers an array of high-quality information and interactive tools to help you and your family manage your daily personal health. The Library has information to fit each individual's needs, whether you choose Health Topics A-Z or Drug Directory. From basic information to advanced health-care topics to What My Doctor Reads on the latest medical trends, CBSHealth-Watch.com brings you the right information at the right time. Become a HealthWatch member—it's free—so you can personalize this site to your wants and needs.

www.LaurusHealth.com

VHA, Inc., a national network of more than 1,800 community-owned hospitals, developed this site. They wanted to provide consumers with a comprehensive, one-stop source of reliable and current health information. When clicked, the general categories of Health News, Health Topics, and Healthy Living give way to additional menu items. Choosing from their popular Health Topics list you'll find information, articles, and data separated into sections like Medical Tests or Illness and Conditions.

www.DrKoop.com

Dr. C. Everett Koop, the former U.S. Surgeon General, believes that people should be empowered to better manage their personal health with comprehensive, trusted information. DrKoop.com strives to be that complete source of consumer health-care information using resources provided by established sources such as Reuters, the National Institutes of Health, the American Cancer Society, and the Koop Institute. One exceptional tool is Drug Checker. You can check your own existing drug prescriptions for potential interactions with over-the-counter drugs or with certain foods and supplements. Use the drug checker every time you begin taking a new medication. Click on Community and find over fifty chat rooms and message boards.

www.MentalHealth.com

Internet Mental Health is an encyclopedia of mental health information for anyone who has an interest in mental health. In a partnership between Canada and Japan, MentalHealth.com is designed for mental health professionals, patients who want to learn more about their illness, friends and families of patients, and anyone who wants to learn more about mental health. Click on Disorders to find the fifty-four most common mental disorders with description, diagnosis, treatment, and research findings included for each one. Click on Internet Links to find additional informational Web sites on specific disorders to help in the understanding of mental health issues, such as ADD, Alzheimer's, and more. You'll also find translations of information into five other languages.

www.MEDLINEplus.gov

This site provides up-to-date, quality health-care information from the world's largest medical library, the National Library of Medicine at the National Institutes of Health. MEDLINEplus.com is for anyone that has a medical question; both health-care professionals and consumers like ourselves can depend on it for accurate, current medical information. Type in a keyword, such as the name of an ailment, a prescription name, or a medical term, and do a search. Click on Health Topics and find a list of topics by general groups, or use the convenient alphabet to select the first letter of your topic. Click on Drug Information for a guide to more than nine thousand prescription and over-the-counter medications.

www.cdc.gov

The Centers for Disease Control and Prevention (CDC), located in Atlanta, Georgia, is an agency of the Department of Health and Human Services. Their mission is to promote health and quality of life by preventing and controlling disease, injury, and disability. If you're planning a trip somewhere, click on Travelers' Health and choose your destination. CDC.com has put together a terrific up-to-date collage of information regarding possible outbreaks of disease or other issues to be aware of. Sections include Traveling with Children, Vaccinations, and Safe Food and Water. Click on Health Topics A-Z for fact sheets and information. Check out their section on Hoaxes and Rumors for a list of current health-related rumors and the CDC's investigative findings.

www.healthfinder.gov

This is a gateway to reliable consumer health and human services information. The site was developed by the U.S. Department of Health and Human Services with information gathered from agencies such as Administration on Aging (AOA), Administration for Children and Families (ACF), and many others. The homepage offers you categories such as Hot Topics and Smart Choices (of health prevention and self-care). Just for You breaks down into age groups of infants through seniors and provides information relevant to each age group. Click on More Tools to use the online databases and medical dictionaries.

Online Pharmacies and Prescription Drug Information

Don't you hate to have to run to the drugstore in the rain because you've run out of something? How would you like the drugstore to deliver over-the-counter health aid supplies and personal beauty products right to your mailbox or door? There are many online drugstores ready and willing to help you keep cough syrups and Band-Aids on hand and available without leaving the comfort of home.

Watch for specials and discount sales at the various drugstore sites, as you would watch the newspaper sale ads. A bargain's a bargain, whether it's free shipping on your first order or a 10-percent-off-anything-in-the-store-this-week-only promotion. Sometimes they offer a buy one, get one free sale. Most sites will keep a reminder shopping list for you of what you've bought in the past, so all you have to do is mark off the items to be replenished; they will then ship them to you within the next few days. You have choices to make; some sites carry more brand items than others.

There are also a couple of sites to check out prescription medicines and read up on interactions with other medications and possible side effects.

www.WebRx.com

WebRx is a full-service drugstore—they call themselves the Health Superstore—that combines the convenience and privacy of online shopping with a tremendous product selection and discount prices. They stock more than twenty-thousand items in departments such as Beauty and Spa, Non-prescription Drugs, and Vitamins and Supplements; easy-to-use tabs show you the way. WebRx.com accepts a wide variety of insurance plans on prescription items. They offer shopping cart comparisons by showing you the prices of items in your cart compared to other online sites when you click on the

Shopping Cart Comparison button found on the left sidebar of each page. Auto Reorder of selected items is available for your convenience.

www.Drugstore.com

A retail online store, Drugstore.com is also an information site for health, beauty, wellness, personal care, and pharmacy products. It offers a licensed pharmacy in relation with Rite Aid. Customers can order prescription drugs online for same-day pickup at a local Rite Aid drugstore. Check out the Living Well Store for benefits of Drugstore.com's relationship with GNC, which gives it the exclusive right to be the online provider of GNC-brand products. At that special time of year, click on the Holiday Store for stocking stuffers and gift ideas packaged for him or her, or check out the top ten gift list.

www.Rx.com

An online licensed pharmacy, Rx.com is compliant with pharmacy regulations in all fifty states, the District of Columbia, and Puerto Rico. It offers the kind of health and medical advice and information you'd expect from your neighborhood pharmacist. It concentrates more on health information and products than just providing another store full of shampoos and deodorants. Click on Prescription Counter to set up your account with insurance information. For prescription prices, you can click on the first letter of the medication and search the list of brand names. Reference Desk will provide Drug Factsheets and health guides for your convenience.

www.Sav-OnDrugs.com

One of the nation's largest food and drug retailers is now online and offers a wide assortment of general merchandise, health and beauty aids, and over-the-counter medications. Membership registration is free. Pharmacy customers from different stores such as Lucky, Jewel Osco, Acme Markets, Sav-on, and Osco Drug Stores can now order prescription refills and check the status of a refill order online. Use Ask the Pharmacist to ask questions by e-mail regarding your medications or over-the-counter products. Check out the Sav-On Specials and Bonus Buys often.

www.RPSPharmacy.com

The AARP Pharmacy Service from Retired Persons Services, Inc. is now online. For clarification, Retired Persons Services, Inc. is a separate, tax-paying entity not owned or controlled by AARP or it affiliates. RPS pays a license fee for use of the AARP name and logo in connection with the AARP Pharmacy Service. Amounts paid to AARP by RPS are used for general purposes of the AARP and its members. RPS was created to serve the members of AARP by providing quality prescription and nonprescription medications and other health-care products in a convenient, low-cost manner.

www.CVS.com

Did you know the first CVS store in 1963 was called "Consumer Value Store"? They now bring the quality and customer service you've known in CVS stores online. You can browse under Shopping Aisles in categories such as Health & Wellness, Household Needs, Photo Center, and more. Under Healthier Living find WebMD.com Web site information and articles. Click on Pharmacy Counter for prescriptions, refills, and advice. Refill Reminders by e-mail are a special personalized feature.

www.RxList.com

At RxList.com you can type in the name of the drug you have questions about and receive a detailed analysis of the substance along with the choice of clicking additional selections such as side effects or drug interactions. Please note the language of this site is more technical than consumer friendly. You can search the RxList.com database for brand name, generic name, and pharmacologic category of a prescription. You can also do an ID or Imprint search, which can be helpful if you've ever dropped your pills on the floor. You'll notice many tablets or capsules have alphanumeric characters printed on them. Use this search to identify by the characters printed (imprint codes) on tablets and capsules to find out what they are. RxList.com also offers the full *Taber's Medical Encyclopedia* of more than fifty-three thousand medical terms for your use.

Nutrition and Exercise

Health and fitness are important for both our grandchildren and ourselves. You can't play and enjoy the children if you're sick or aching. Likewise, good nutrition benefits us all.

www.eFit.com

A diet and exercise site, eFit.com will encourage you each day with positive nudges. Personalized for every member, eFit.com will devise an exercise and nutritional program, offer you dozens of weekly articles that relate to your goals, provide thousands of video demonstrations to ensure you're doing everything right, and help you locate whatever you need to stick to your program, from yoga classes and swimming pools to vegetarian restaurants and heart-rate monitors. They'll even hook you up with other eFit members for team training and support. For a more intense program, you can choose a customized diet program in which, for a fee, you will have your own personal coach/nutritionist for four weeks. You'll receive a personalized nutritional profile with daily menus.

www.NutritionFitness.com

If you eat right and get in shape, you'll feel better and live longer. Use NutritionFitness.com's Body Mass Index calculator to find out your factor of fitness. It only takes a few seconds, and they'll explain the results to you. Click on Nutrition for a list of general nutrition topics from anorexia to menopause. Click on Fitness to find information on the benefits from exercising and yoga. You can receive a weekly newsletter to your e-mail address from their online nutritionist.

www.WeightDirectory.com

This Web site is a portal to weight-loss products and services as well as to chat rooms and support groups to help you lose weight and get in shape. The homepage regularly lists new information and articles with quick headlines you can browse. Check out New Sites for a continually updated database of fitness and weight-loss information. Click on Kids & Teens for sites related to the younger group for nutrition and weight loss.

www.LongerLiving.com

Is this an answer to aging? Possibly. The articles and information point you in the right direction to good health. This new and growing Web site concentrates on giving you healthy, accurate information. Click on Active Living for an article about fitness or exercise. Did you know there's a low-impact activity called "Spinning," or group indoor biking?

www.WorkoutsForWomen.com

You can enjoy fitness tips and instructions from the home-page. Click on the Exercise Spotlight for an easy how-to for a particular movement. However, WorkoutsForWomen.com's main objective is to offer personal training programs online exclusively for women. You receive weekly home exercise programs via online video/audio presentation with written descriptions and unlimited e-mail consultations with Joni Hyde, a trainer certified by the prestigious American College of Sports Medicine. Memberships are as low as three dollars a week.

www.DeepSlowEasy.com

The Deep Slow and Easy fitness program is a free online cyber-exercise system. On this site created by Rick Davids (click on Biography), you'll find breathing exercises to reduce stress and increase good health. Click on Try It! Rick talks about how we only breathe shallowly at the computer. Shallow breathing deprives our lungs, our muscles, and our brain the air they need for health. Click on Start and he takes you through the steps for deep, slow breathing. Click on More Exercises for a choice of a series of seventeen or nine stretching and strengthening exercises. Read the Advice page for tips and information.

www.RiverMaya.com

Yoga is a holistic system for unifying the body, mind, and spirit. Ultimately it results in well-being, peace, and bliss. This is how RiverMaya.com starts you on a journey of relaxation and meditation. Three choices—Meditation, Exercises, and Breathing—are listed at the bottom of the homepage. Click on each one to receive tips and information on yoga. Want a moment of tranquillity in a busy day? Click on the circles at the top of the pages. Each one fills your screen with a photo of serenity and you'll hear beautiful background music. Take a few deep breaths and enjoy.

www.JustWalk.com

We all know exercise is an important component to a healthy lifestyle, but we don't always get around to it. JustWalk.com offers you a free exercise tracking system to keep you motivated in reaching your fitness goals through walking. Simply enter the date and duration of your walking, and you'll be able to see reports and graphs of your efforts. Use JustWalk.com to track your exercise, compare your work with other users of Just Walk, get feedback, and motivate yourself.

Diet Information

If you think you've tried every known-to-man diet, you haven't checked on the Internet. Do a search on the word "diet," and you'll be amazed at the international gamut of Web sites designed to help you lose weight. Be aware that anyone can set up a Web site on any subject. That doesn't make one an expert nor does it mean that the program is healthy and safe. Eating nothing but twelve sticks of bubblegum a day will not put you in the perfect size 10 dress. Be rational in your quest for good health.

www.WeightWatchers.com

Weight Watchers is an internationally known weight-loss organization. Its homepage opens with a map of the world. Click on the United States. You can check out Weight Watchers' latest system for losing or maintaining your weight, as well as healthy recipes and tips.

www.RichardSimmons.com

One of my favorite Web sites is about the delightful weight-loss guru, Richard Simmons. He stole my lethargic heart back in the 1970s when I was a working mom trying to survive. You have to smile when you see this tank-topped guy wearing short shorts; you can't help it. He is such a love, full of energy and enthusiasm. He has a Web site filled with tips and tricks, recipes and encouragement.

He'll help you to stay your healthiest through an eating plan. Check it out for simple, effective information. You can join his club and be one of thousands of women dedicated to feeling better about life and about themselves.

www.AtkinsCenter.com

Information regarding the famous Dr. Atkins' low-carbohydrate diet can be found at this site, as well as Dr. Atkins products and retail outlets. What is the Atkins Diet? The Atkins Diet restricts processed and/or refined carbohydrates (which can make up over 50 percent of many people's diets) such as high-sugar foods, breads, pasta, cereal, and starchy vegetables. A complete online catalog lists supplements and products with shopping cart convenience.

www.JennyCraig.com

JennyCraig.com gives you the opportunity to experience some of the tools available in the current Jenny Craig Weight Loss Programs, find new ways to balance your life in their Resource Center, find support buddies in the message boards, or shop in the eJenny store filled with great cookbooks and support tools.

www.TOPS.org

TOPS, Take Off Pounds Sensibly, has been around for more than fifty years. They offer a healthy, caring, and supportive approach to weight control at an affordable price. You do not need to be a member to enjoy most of the tips and information on this Web site. Members meet weekly to aid in attaining and maintaining your weight goals through group support. Click on Chapter Locator and enter your zip code for a group near you.

www.DietWatch.com

As one of the first virtual diet centers on the Internet, DietWatch.com offers personalized support with a free daily diary and informational support as a Web-based community of dieters. Enrollment is free. Click on Diet Reviews for information to help you decide which diet is right for you. Check out some of their success stories in the Guided Tour. DietWatch.com is monitored by health-care professionals and complies with the HON-code principles of the Health on the Net Foundation.

www.CyberDiet.com

On this site, nutritional information, discussion and chat groups for support, and interactive tools help you with your weight-loss goals. Click on Self-Assessment for a list of tools to help you get started. Want to know your waist-to-hip ratio (WHR)? What's a good target heart rate for your age? This site offers simple, easy-to-use tools to increase your awareness of where you are (physically) right now and where you want to be in the future. Now check out Diet And Nutrition, and go into a variety of choices, such as Fast Food Quest, Dining Out, and Recipe Makeovers. Check out the user-friendly Fast Food Quest, an excellent source of nutritional information on most of the national chains such as Arby's, Burger King, and Kentucky Fried Chicken.

www.DietersClub.com

This is an e-mail support group. At DietersClub.com, you'll find women who are trying to diet, dieting, or maintaining their weight loss. They share tips, advice, recipes, and all-around support. Motivating each other is a primary goal. Scroll to the bottom of the homepage and you can click on Members' Intros for an example of the women who have joined this Web site. Check out Diet/Exercise Tips. A one-time fee of five dollars is required once you've agreed to join.

www.LosingItOnline.com

Meet Melody Jo, the founder and Webmaster of LosingItOnline. She has created a free weight loss support community. Click on How To Reach Your Goal to read sound advice on the four essentials of any weight-loss program: good attitude, exercise, water, and portion control. Use the Monthly Challenge to log in your efforts and record your results. Click on Message Board to see how other women are doing and to reach out for your own support.

Times weren't all that easy when we were growing up; let your grandchildren know about life before polio vaccinations or fluoride. Okay, we didn't come over on the Mayflower, but we didn't have seventeen different flavors of toothpaste either. To our grandchildren, that makes us practically ancient. Help them appreciate the medical miracles available today that were almost unimaginable before.

What's a grandmother to do to help provide a happy and safe environment for her grandchildren? Stay informed. Find out and stand out. As a grandmother, the children may listen to you more than their parents. You have the power to pass on to the younger generations advice on how to stay healthy and active in this busy world of ours. And then take that sage advice for yourself. Take care of yourself, you're worth it.

That's Entertainment

We may have to grow old, but we can refuse to grow up. Have you seen the bumper sticker "It's never too late to have a happy childhood"? Be that bumper sticker. Take a walk in the rain. Stop and smell the flowers along the path of life. We used to be little girls. Bobby socks and pigtails, we were splash-in-the-puddle kind of people. Then we grew up and had responsibilities.

Well, we're the grandmothers now. It's okay to play—and who better to share the concept of "okay to play" with than the grandchildren?

Show them what your childhood was like once upon a time. The newest generation is always curious about the fact that someone they love, that they see as old, could have been a little girl. Snuggle together on the couch on a rainy afternoon and tell them stories of the days when you were their age and what life was like. Don't miss an opportunity to share with them a piece of history, and it is historical to them. I know we don't like to think of ourselves as old, but to the under-ten crowd, we are right up there with other famous people they hear about: George Washington, Betsy Ross—you know, those people.

Music and Song Lyrics

Did your grandmother use to hum tunes while doing the dishes? My voice blends with the short people around me as we sing whole choruses of Disney songs in the car or

"We Just Figured Out Blue's Clues" while making a mess in the kitchen. Don't worry; after you've watched *The Lion King* for the three hundredth time, you'll know all the words to "Hakuna Matata."

We learned songs in elementary school from some book with a broken binding during the afternoon choral practice. "My Grandfather's Clock" and the "Erie Canal" come to mind. It didn't matter if we sang with a piano or a cappella, there would still sometimes be harmonizing.

www.Mudcat.org

The Mudcat Café is a magazine dedicated to blues and folk music. Mudcat.org has a lyric database of over eight thousand songs; see if you can find the words to a favorite folk song. To ensure the spirit and knowledge of traditional music is passed down from generation to generation, they created The Mudcat Café for Kids. It provides animated folk tales, lyrics to children's songs, and activities such as Make Your Own Instruments.

www.bbhq.com

Bbhq.com is building a collection of lyrics to some of the best and most interesting songs of the fifties, sixties, and early to mid-seventies. Its purpose is to bring back some memories, perhaps settle a few bets, and allow our grand-kids to compare the words of our songs to the lyrics of what passes for rock and roll today. Click on The Music

Room from the homepage. Click on Lyrics and scan down to the lower portion of the page to see the songs in alphabetical order by title.

www.Disney.com

Are show tunes and Disney tunes too tame for your little guys? Grandma's gotta be cool and hip; find out the difference between boy bands like the Backstreet Boys, 'NSync, and 98°. Crank up Radio Disney on your computer and find out Dean Martin has been replaced in the hearts of the younger generations with Ricky Martin. From Disney's homepage click on Disney's Club Blast to find the Radio Disney icon. You can click Listen and it will play the radio station broadcast right from your computer speakers. You'll learn who's hot and who's not in tunesville for the preteen generation.

www.Kidscom.com

Let your grandchild make up a song. Click on Just For Fun, scroll down, and click on Skeeter's Music Machine. You find a virtual piano keyboard with eight notes that you play by using your mouse. When your grandchild is ready, click Record and have them play out the new melody. Click Stop. Click Play Back to hear your young maestro's concerto over and over till you click Stop.

www.lyrics.ch

Click on the big yellow oval that reads lyrics.ch. They have collected a database of over sixty-two thousand songs. You can type in the artist, the album name, or the song title. Click Find Songs for a listing. The words to the song may be copyrighted, and it will allow you to view them, but not to print them.

www.SheetMusicPlus.com

With over a quarter of a million titles, you can find just about any piece of sheet music you would like to buy on this site. Start by clicking on Search All Music or Search Classical Music on the homepage, or start with any underlined link. This will take you to a search tool for the category you picked. Use the text boxes and pop-up menus in the search tool to describe either the title of the song or the artist, then click the Find It! button. This takes you to a page listing products that match your description. Shopping cart convenience is available for purchasing your items online.

www.Kareoke.com

Click on History to find that *karaoke* is an abbreviated compound word: "kara" comes from the Japanese word *karappo* meaning "empty," and "oke" is an abbreviation of *okesutura*, a word for "orchestra." A recorded song consists of both vocals and accompaniment. Music tapes in which only the accompaniment is recorded were called *karaoke*. Most English-speaking people pronounce the word as "kar-e-oke," and since practically everything on the Internet is "e-something," Kareoke.com just seemed right. You can buy songs from this site, or click Sing Kareoke Now and start belting out your favorite tune.

www.EatSleepMusic.com

Want to be a diva? *Karaoke* can be found at this site where you can sing in the comfort and privacy of your own home. The music can be selected with or without accompanying vocals. The words will appear on your screen a few lines at a time, and will change colors to keep you focused on where you are in the song.

Games for Kids

When your grandchildren come over to visit, whether it is on school vacation or every other Saturday, there are sites on the Internet where you can play games together. Remember our motto: It's okay to play. These are colorful, animated sites you play for free—a video arcade in your own home.

I must warn you before challenging your little heartthrob to a computer game, be sure you have practiced using your mouse or track ball. Do you feel comfortable using it in quick point-and-click rhythms?

What about doing the point, click, and drag procedure, where you hold down the left mouse button while you drag an icon from one spot to another? You are going to need to be somewhat proficient in these skills for various games, and children seem to pick up the concepts by magic.

Get a comfortable chair for yourself (you may be there a while) and a chair for your grandchild. Get yourselves close to the keyboard and mouse. Let the games begin.

www.MamaMedia.com

This site is graphic intensive, which means it may take a while to come up on your screen, both initially as well as when you move to different sections within the site. Be patient; it is worth the wait. Again you need to register, but it's free. Click on Play to view the four main kid-centered sections: Surprise, Romp, Buzz, and Zap. Click on Surprise, and you're in a gaming section. Check out the Riddle Machine with child-sized riddles that come with their own laugh track when you click on the answer. Click the Send in a Riddle button for your grandchildren to submit their favorite riddle for publication. You may have to type it in for them. MamaMedia.com has a grown-ups area you can click into before the grandkids arrive and learn what each of the games and areas do. This is an especially nice feature. It gives you step-by-step instructions and advice on its "Webtivities." Be ready for the eagerness and energy the little ones will have to play with their grandma on the computer.

www.CrayolaKids.com

From the makers of Crayola crayons, this Web site comes with project ideas, trivia, and puzzles. Click on Activity Book for crafts and print-out pages to color. Click on Crayola Census for information and a chance to vote on your favorite color in the box. Send a Crayola e-greeting card under Create a Card. Take a virtual tour of the Crayola Factory in Pennsylvania; click on the floor map and see how crayons are made.

www.Yucky.com

Yucky.com is for a little older crowd, maybe six years old and up. The site is based on games and real information with a slime, worm, or yucky concept. Just what kids love most, stuff that gives us grandmothers the shivers. Click on Yucky Fun & Games for exciting games like Toxic Waste and X-Terminate. Or play Speed Zone where you try to repeat a pattern of flashing lights that gradually speeds up and becomes more complicated. Gross and Cool Body gives grandchildren kid-friendly answers to their questions about human body functions. Remember the name of this site is Yucky.com; it lives up to it.

www.Shockwave.com

Here's a Web site for preteens and teenage grandchildren with more developed hand-eye coordination. At Shockwave.com, they take fun seriously. You'll find games, music, and puzzles. Click on Games and find subheadings for Arcade Classics (popular video games from the 1980s), Arcade Action, Sports, and others. The older kids will probably know what to do, but each one comes with play instructions for us grandmothers. I stress "older" grandchildren only for this site because some of the activities are rated PG-13, such as games with the South Park cartoon characters or deer hunting under Sports.

www.Bonus.com

The Super Site for Kids is fun and energetic. Click Play to find a variety of choices for any imagination. Choose from over a dozen headings such as Word Games, Mazes, Arcade, or Sports. Each of those has a menu of games to offer, enough to keep little fingers busy for a long, long time. And that's just under Play. You still have Imagine, New Fun, Explore, and Color to check out. Each one has just as many options—and variety of fun for all ages and energy levels.

www.KidsDomain.com

Kid's Domain is a kid-oriented site, created by a staff of parents, with fun stuff for kids to make, do, and see. The site is updated and/or expanded weekly, so you'll want to return often. There are games, contests, crafts, and holiday pages with fun activities. Click on Kids for a menu of options such as Pokémon, Online Games, and Brain Builders. Each one will give you a list of games and activities. Although the site specializes in an age range of two through twelve, there is enough offered in all skill levels and activities for the big kid in all of us.

www.Kids-Space.org

Kids' Space has three main sections for young children. Kids' Gallery is a showcase for art submitted by young users. The Gallery has many subjects such as Fantasy or People. Click on one and you see the themes and a menu of rooms to enter. Click on the door icons and visit the works. Click on the artist's name for an enlargement of his or her creative project. Go back to the homepage and try Storybook, where there are shelves containing stories about kids, by kids, for kids. The last main section is Beanstalk, where children can submit stories about art they've seen in the Gallery or draw a picture for a story they've read in Storybook. The site has quality concepts and easy-to-follow instructions for submittal. Also note that this site is commercial free, which is quite refreshing.

www.Claus.com

'Twas the night before Christmas—no, that's another story. But a visit to this delightful North Pole is available online. Visit Santa Claus and the North Pole Village, which is full of fun things to do for both kids and parents. Each building represents a fun activity or project. Check your Naughty or Nice rating by typing in your name. Check out the Top Ten Ways to Make the Naughty List; some of them apply to us adults too. Play a variety of holiday games in Elf School and print your own Honorary Elf Diploma when you're finished. In Elf School the important thing is to have fun: Sing along with new original Christmas songs. Try funny holiday recipes. Visit the amazing Toy Workshop. Send an e-mail to Santa Claus. With colorful illustrations, this site is a creative family experience for young and old. Claus.com is one of the top-rated Santa Claus Web sites and is known around the world.

www.KidAuthors.com

KidAuthors.com is a creative place for kids like your grandchildren to share their stories and poems with people around the world, including your friends and family. Read together the stories and poems written by kids from around the world. Click on Submit a Story and you not only get a chance to write your own tale of adventure, but you also get to choose a color for the text and a background color. How fun. Click on one of the categories under Stories and find a list with the title, author's name, and comments.

www.GusTown.com

Meet Gus, a dog from CyberTime, and his friends, the CyberBuds, at this fun site. Click on one of the buildings in GusTown and enjoy a variety of activities. Check out the Library where you can meet Rae. Finish a story that Rae has started about the CyberBuds and you may find yours posted in the Library. Click on the Post Office and you can send a letter to Gus and his friends. At the Café you can check out recipes in the kitchen or Web sites from clicking on the bulletin board. At the Toy Store you can click on Cyber Games and play online, or you can click on the T-shirts and purchase software for your home computer.

HUMOR AND JOKES

CuteStuf.com is a great source for laughter and fun. Some of the most hilarious goofiness on the Net is here for all ages to enjoy. If you are looking for clean funny pictures, stupid jokes, cute cartoons, virtual greeting cards, and other silly stuff, this is the place. Each of their funny pictures comes with an e-mail address form to send it on to your friends if you want to share. Seasonal and new greetings will be added often. You will find loads of quality humor to keep you laughing daily.

www.GotLaughs.com

Since 1999, GotLaughs.com has provided Internet users with funny pictures, jokes, comics, and cartoons. Again, if you find something that really tickles your funny bone, this site offers you an e-mail address form to send it on to your friends. Jokes and pictures are updated often for seasonal or newsworthy happenings. Sign up for their daily e-mail and you'll have a smile a day delivered to your inbox.

www.gcfl.net

Good Clean Funnies List is a Web page and mailing list for sending out one good, clean joke a day, five days a week. If you enjoy a joke in the morning before the start of your day, you will love gcfl.com. Share them with your family and friends. Here's an example of their humor: "Mid-life can bring out your angry, bitter side. You look at your latte-swilling, beeper-wearing know-it-all twenty-something child and think, 'For this I have stretch marks?'"

www.glasbergen.com

Check out Today's Cartoon for a fresh look at life today. Randy Glasbergen's daily cartoons are sure to bring a smile to your face. His talent is seen in national magazines and newspapers. Scroll down the screen for the day's cartoon. Continue scrolling to see the past week's archive. Further down the site, you'll find Randy's cartoons separated into categories such as Diet, Health and Fitness, and Marriage and Relationships. Once you click on a category, continue scrolling down the screen to see cartoon after great cartoon.

www.itsajoke.com

The homepage on this site is less hectic than most. You have four main sections to choose from. When you click on Funny Pictures, you see a list of thumbnail-sized pictures. Click on it once to enlarge the photo and read the cute punch line. You can e-mail these to your friends if you'd like. Cool Jokes has categories of Family Related and Senior Citizen.

www.funnycleanjokes.com

Funny Clean Jokes pokes good-natured fun at dumb blondes, rednecks, family life, lawyers, men and women, and politicians. Easy-to-use tabs across the top will take you to Cartoons or Odds and Ends. They update the Front Page jokes daily. There are hundreds of good funny clean jokes in seventeen categories in a searchable archive.

Games for Grandma

Want to play something a little more challenging as an adult while the grandchildren are away from your computer? There are games sites for us grandmothers, too, which include board games and card games. Think of it as an exercise in using your mouse. You are gaining computer skills and proficiency by point-and-clicks during each game. Ease the stress of a busy week by giving yourself a chance to play. Win or lose, you're sure to have a great time.

www.BingoBugle.com

You can play free bingo, twenty-four hours a day, seven days a week. Just register for your free account, and you can start the action for great prizes. The same people that publish a bingo tabloid newspaper that is found free in most bingo halls bring this online bingo site to you. BingoBugle.com has several different types of bingo games to choose from. Players can earn Bugle$ while playing and redeem them for merchandise or cash. BingoBugle.com offers other features. Check out Aunt Bingo and her advice column, Rumors (the daily news of major bingo happenings), Comics, and links for additional Web sites.

www.acbl.com

For the serious bridge player, check out the American Contract Bridge League. This site provides quite a bit of information as well as links to clubs nationwide. Click on the selection bar for more topics. You can become a member for an annual fee, which entitles you to *Bridge* magazine, discounted entry fees into tournament play, access to more than thirty-five hundred North American bridge clubs, and more.

www.iWin.com

One of the most popular free gaming sites on the Net has all kinds of card games. Check out their Top Ten Games List, or click on Games at the top of the homepage for an index of free games available. By playing games at iWin.com you accumulate icoins, which can be exchanged for chances to win cash and prizes. Prizes you can win are listed on the homepage. New games are added frequently so come back often.

www.Pogo.com

Here is one of the leading online game sites. Pogo.com offers familiar, popular, easy-to-use games in a variety of selections such as casino, trivia, and arcade. Register for free with a unique user name, then choose your game. You will be playing these games with people all over the world! Whether you want a leisurely social game or are vying to be world champ, click on The Classics to find your favorite card and board games. Or check out Wordopolis. For hundreds of word-wranglers ready to wrap their minds around these brain-stumpers, Pogo.com offers crossword and word search. The puzzles change every day, so come back early and often.

www.Gamesville.com

From the people at Lycos, the search engine, comes Gamesville.com. You can either click on a listed card game or bingo play, or look under Sports and find the Lycos Game Listing. Click on the Listing and find thousands of gaming sites to choose from. Simply set up your free user name; it costs nothing to play any of their games. Since you never wager, bet, risk, or lose anything, technically you're not gambling.

www.Uproar.com

An interactive entertainment area for grown-ups is online for you. Click first on Games, then click on Board/Tile Games to play the ancient game of Mah Jong or a version of Mah Jong Solitaire. Or click on Card Games to play different versions of solitaire or to play against the computer in exciting games of Gin Rummy or Hearts. Don't forget to check out Puzzles.

www.Games.com

Brought to you by its parent company, Hasbro, Inc., Games.com is one of the newest game sites on the Net. Games like Monopoly, Scrabble, Risk, Asteroids, chess, Centipede, backgammon, hearts, and others are offered, most of which will be multiplayer. You'll be able to play Monopoly, for example, with up to six other players from around the world. All of the multiplayer games have a chat feature, so you can swap tips and strategies with other players, or just talk about the weather. And when you just want to play, there are great solo-play games like Asteroids, solitaire, and Scrabble Blitz. Games.com also offers tournaments, tips, and articles about games, all aimed at offering players a community around their favorite games. Check out their online store, to make finding and purchasing some of the best games a snap. They'll be continually adding new games, contests, and other game-related content to Games.com, so there will always be something new to try.

www.webMillion.com

Here's a chance to play a daily lottery system for millions. Once you register, you have ten chances a day, choosing six numbers per lottery pick, to qualify for the weekly drawing. Plus every day you can play an assortment of games such as Trivia and Click 3. Mixed-Up is a word scramble game and Hang Million is a version of the word game Hangman for a chance at more prizes. It's free, it's fun.

Where do I go for a break when stress or tensions are needling me? I enjoy clicking into the Margaritaville room and playing Ali Baba with some really great people at Pogo.com. I'm sure to find my smile again chatting with the likes of CJ and Pi (not their real monikers), celebrating October 4 birthdays, or getting virtual hugs from Okie and Cyber. I have found fellow Washington neighbors, Joy and Paul. It doesn't take long before I'm lol (laughing out loud) over the antics and comments, besides trying to win the jackpot. Sometimes going for the gold isn't the most important part of the process. Hey, roomies, I'll brb (be right back).

ONLINE CASINOS

Not many of us are located near hot beds of bright lights and slot machines—and that could be a good thing. Atlantic City, Las Vegas, and Reno can be quite expensive. How would you like to play your favorite casino games without having to dress up or spend money? Slots, blackjack, roulette wheels, and video poker are waiting for you on various Web sites. I encourage you to enjoy and stay with the free casino sites or free play within a game. Ignore the advertising of those sites that will charge you to play or have you gamble real dollars from your credit card.

www.bigprizes.com

BigPrizes.com has a simple concept: You play games, earn points, and then you submit your points to win prizes. Become a member for free. Play the Jukebox slot machine for a chance to win fabulous prizes, such as an iMac personal computer or a gift certificate from Ice.com, the diamond jewelry people, instantly. Otherwise build your points toward a prize of your choice. You also compete for a cash grand prize.

www.Pogo.com

Play their casino games for cash jackpots—for free. Each game has a cash jackpot waiting for some lucky winner. Play keno, video poker, roulette, and blackjack. Enjoy chatting with others while you play. When someone makes a great run or hits a large prize, the other people in your casino room become supportive with wtg (way to go) and congratulations. The cash jackpots are progressive; as soon as someone wins, the jackpot starts building again.

Fun.casino.com

Meet Johnny B. Slick and his casino games. They are free, fun, and have been developed in Shockwave format so that you can enjoy them on your computer. Since there's no real money at stake, you can practice your strategies in video poker, blackjack, and craps at no risk.

For your convenience, most of the portal sites such as iWon.com or NBCi.com have a gaming section using Pogo.com's casino rooms. Your registration on Pogo.com will not work at these other sites and vice versa. If you are signed up at iWon.com, you'll need a new identity at Pogo.com. Most people just add an underscore (_) to their name to make it different. Example: if you are browneyes on one site, try brown_eyes at the other.

Toys

Do you remember when the Mattel or Hasbro companies were brand-new? Maybe your parents only had the choice between buying a porcelain-faced baby doll or a picture book for your Christmas or Hanukkah surprise, or your holiday gifts were handmade rather than bought from a store. Share these stories with your grandchildren. Explain to them that tic-tac-toe was a game before they were born and long before it became a television game show called

Hollywood Squares. Tell them you were one of the jump-rope greats in your fourth grade class. If your grandchildren are out of the area, write these stories down and send them in packets of snail mail. Don't let time slip away without sharing your school days with them.

When it comes time to buy a present for your grandchild, toy shopping has never been easier or more fun. Let your grandchildren show you what their latest gotta-have items are, and learn about the newest fads in toy town. What's hot and what's not for kids of all ages is available on the Internet.

www.Mattel.com

In 1945, Mattel began operations out of a garage workshop. The original founders, Harold Matson and Elliot Handler, coined the company name by combining letters of their last and first names, respectively. (Matson later sold out to the Handlers.) In 1955, in a move that would revolutionize the way toys were marketed, Mattel bought fifty-two weeks of advertising on the new Mickey Mouse Club television show, marking the first time toys had been advertised on a year-round basis. In 1959, Mattel introduced Barbie. Inspired by her daughter's fascination with cutout adult paper dolls, Ruth Handler suggested making a three-dimensional doll through which little girls could act out their dreams. She named the doll "Barbie," which was the nickname of her real-life daughter.

www.ToyClassics.com

Would you believe there's a grandparent's site for toy buying? Well, this is it. The category names are delightful. Look for banks under A Penny Saved. Check out Down Memory Lane for toys you may have grown up with, such as wooden stilts or a book on cat's cradle string games. Out of the variety of topics to choose from, click on Grandparent/Family, which includes terrific clothing ideas for us with stock grandmother names to have printed. Order a sweatshirt with Grammy, Nana, or Grandma, just for you. There's even a family tree necklace with ceramic tiles for each grandchild. Don't forget to click on Grandma's Bargain Basement for discounted toys and deals.

www.FisherPrice.com

Toys. Lots of toys at FisherPrice.com. You can click on Toys by Age, Toys by Type, Toys that Teach, Character Toys, or do a search. At the bottom of every toy's description page is a link to a retail store locator, which lists retailers that carry Fisher-Price products within a specified distance from your home zip code. For your convenience, they also have their catalog online where you can purchase toys and clothing and have them shipped directly to you or your grandchildren. Then click on Make Playtime Count from the homepage and get age-specific tips on bonding and encouraging life skills such as self-confidence and problem solving.

www.HotWheels.com

How did little cars become such a hot item, decade after decade? You can click on Kids' Only to visit a virtual collection of cars or airplanes, or play games. Sign your grandchildren up at the Birthday Club. HotWheels.com will send a birthday card and a coupon for a free Hot Wheels car on their special day. Then click on The Hot Wheels Shop from the homepage and purchase online track sets, play sets, or a selection of their die-cast cars. Click on Wish List and let the grandchildren help you enter which products they most desire.

www.Barbie.com

Yes, Barbie even has her own Web site. From her colorful homepage, you can get sidetracked into playing games, checking out the latest Barbie fashions, or creating your own friend for Barbie. Click on Catalog and you can shop for hours at the Barbie Boutique. In the World of Barbie catalog, kids can look without the worry of purchasing. Dolls and accessories are just the beginning—but what a beginning; choose from holiday Barbies to activity versions like Kitty Fun or Star Splash Barbie. Then you have categories ranging from Stationery and Software, to Clothes and Shoes. Barbie has her own lip-gloss making kit and hair extensions for styling. That doll has everything. A separate section is available on collectibles.

www.Hasbro.com

Hasbro, Inc., started in 1923 as a family-owned company, has grown from eight family members working in a small shop in Providence, Rhode Island, to a children's and family leisure time and entertainment company with approximately ten thousand employees worldwide. Two brothers, Henry and Helal Hassenfeld, founded Hasbro. From Hasbro came Mr. Potato Head, and in 1964 they introduced G.I. Joe. In 1984, they acquired the Milton Bradley company along with Playskool. Check out the Click Here for Recall Information as well.

www.WoodenToy.com

For something a little different, check out this site. John Michael Linck makes beautiful fine toys out of Wisconsin hardwoods. See his beautifully crafted designs of a child's stool, a doll's bed, a block wagon, and a rocking horse. Click on each photo for a complete description. To purchase any of these great items, print out the Wooden Toy Order form. "I want my toys to furnish an alternative to some of the throwaway aspects of life today," says Mr. Linck.

www.ToysRUs.com

ToysRUs.com and Amazon.com have teamed up to provide you with a quality, easy-to-use online toy-shopping experience. ToysRUs.com's vast selection of toys, great deals, and exclusive offers, combined with Amazon.com's super-reliable shipping, delivery, and renowned customer service, means you get the best of all worlds. You can browse through the products by age or by categories. Do a search using keywords. Check out the Top Sellers, a list that is updated hourly. Other features include gift wrapping, gift certificates, and e-mail reminder notices when your grandchildren's birthdays are close.

www.KBKids.com

KB Toys, the nation's largest mall-based specialty toy retailer, is now online with a wide variety of toys, software, video games, and collectibles. Click on Toys. You can browse by Featured Shops, you can shop by age groups, or you can shop by price range. Brand-name toys are divided in a simple drop-down menu. Everything is set up for ease of shopping. Definitely click on Outlet from the homepage or at any time while shopping. Check out their great products at up to 75 percent off. Product items change often, so check back. You can purchase Gift Cards in denominations of fifteen, thirty, and fifty dollars. These will be shipped to you and can be used at any KB Toys or online.

www.ZanyBrainy.com

Zany Brainy, the nation's award-winning retailer of Extraordinary Toys for Extraordinary Kids, is online. With almost two hundred stores across the nation, they pride themselves on having the most comprehensive collection of high-quality, nonviolent, safe, and incredibly fun products for kids. The featured areas are Ages and Stages to shop by specific age, or Browse by Trusted Brand or by Favorite Character. Check out the Zany Exclusives, toys you'll find only at Zany Brainy.

Don't forget to check out the auction sites as well when toy shopping. In the late fifties or early sixties, there was a toy I always wanted but Santa never brought: Mr. Machine was a clear plastic put-together kind of toy that showed how his gears and cogs worked together when he moved. I have bid on the packages that people have carefully hoarded in their attics and closets all this time, but so far I have lost out to higher bidders. I'll keep trying though!

At an auction site, I also found old Colorforms for sale, those wonderful bits of thin plastic in various characters that you could use to make up stories. One of my favorites was Disney's *Sleeping Beauty*. I won that auction, and discovered many timeless memories inside the worn cardboard box that came in the mail. Prince Philip, the three good fairies, and Aurora herself stared back at me from the black, waxed holders.

Amusement Parks

If you have older grandchildren who dream of going on every thriller roller coaster in the United States, you may want to pass that heart-stopping adventure on to their parents. What you can do instead is let them go to the Internet and search for the top ten thriller rides. There are Web sites with all the information on roller coasters they can absorb online. Learn more than you ever wanted to know about the latest and greatest in thrill-seeking rides. Show them what a hip grandmother you are by knowing the difference between Colossus and the Canyon Blaster, without having to prove personal experience. Fasten your seat belts.

www.UltimateRollerCoaster.com

This site provides informative, entertaining, and up-to-date information on roller coasters, thrill rides, and amusement parks in an easy-to-navigate manner. Find out which park has the tallest and fastest rides. Click on Roller Coasters and choose from Ride Reviews, Picture Gallery, or Record Book. Click on News to find out the latest news and happenings at parks around the country.

www.ThrillRide.com

Created by an amusement park expert, ThrillRide.com opens with the sounds of a roller coaster and a fast display of photos. Your menu choices from the homepage include Ride Reviews, Hot News, Wild Rumors, and more. Ride Reviews is exceptional, in details and personal experience essay.

www.RollerCoasterWorld.com

RollerCoasterWorld.com is a source for roller-coaster photos, information, and even items you can purchase. Click on Postcards, then on Vintage Postcards for a look back at some excellent memories. Click on Hersheypark 2000 to find out the first racing/dueling coaster in the United States is called Lightning Racer.

Party Planning and Decorating

Don't wait to celebrate with your grandchild once a year on his or her birthday. You may not be able to attend a birthday party because you live a thousand miles away, but parties do not have to be for birthdays or holidays alone. Be a hero and throw a colorful event any time of the year for your grandchildren.

Your little curly-topped sweetheart lost her first tooth? Throw a tooth fairy party. Your T-ball hero had a great game? Throw a baseball theme party. It's okay to eat off paper plates any time of the year. Just ask your little ones, they'll agree. Want ideas for party themes? Here is a sample of party Web sites:

www.iParty.com

From children's birthday parties to weddings, Super Bowl extravaganzas to Halloween costume parties, iParty.com uses the Internet to make it easy and convenient for you to plan and give fabulous parties. Here you can exchange ideas about parties, select themes, and purchase all of the goods and services for a successful event. Under Party Planning and Supplies, you can choose from drop-down menus under Birthdays, Milestones, Seasonal, or Themes. They even have Parrot Head party supplies under the Specialty Shop. Don't miss the supportive features in their *iParty Talk* magazine.

www.CelebrateExpress.com

CelebrateExpress.com was founded in 1994 by Jan and Mike Jewell after their third child, Sebastian, was born three months premature weighing only 1 lb. 10 oz. They know how precious children are and have created CelebrateExpress.com for busy parents and grandparents to celebrate the lives of their own children. From the homepage, you can click BirthdayExpress.com and choose from over a hundred birthday party themes, or go into

CelebrateExpress.com for all-occasion theme parties. You can click on Piñatas and see a list of choices such as a ruby-red slipper or Madeline's yellow hat. Check out their party-planning guides for tips, recipes, and game ideas.

www.KidsPartyWorld.com

From the inspiration and stress of creating her own children's parties, Florence Baiocchi founded KidsParty-World.com, a one-stop party place. Not only do they offer an array of different party themes and supplies, but they can also help with special party planning in your geographical area. Check out their Party Places and Specialty Acts for locations to put on the perfect party or for entertainers available in your area. Type in your area code and it generates a list of balloon shops, clowns, rent a Moon Bounce, or whatever may be in your region for a great party.

www.Piñatas.com

Click on the Consumer Catalog option for a look at their extensive selection of quality Mexican handmade party piñatas. You can search by category or browse by price range. Under Licensed Piñatas there are NFL helmet- and football-shaped ones. The artwork on the Limited Editions is incredible. Click on Match Any Party Theme to find a generic piñata where you can attach cutouts from your own decorations. Choose Custom Piñatas, and whether it's your team's mascot, your child's favorite fairy-tale character, or something you made up yourself, they can make it into a piñata. Simply e-mail, fax, or mail the image to them for a price quote.

www.eVite.com

Take the Get To Know eVite tour, an easy-to-use, step-by-step instruction on receiving or sending an electronic invitation. Evites can be used for any occasion you can think of. You can add graphics, colors, and sound. Click on Create a Poll to send to your friends or family to find out just about anything. Want to decide about holiday gift exchanging in April? Send a poll to all family members.

www.PartyBiz.com

Here is a one-stop shop for party supplies. Everything you need for any event is professionally designed, coordinated, and delivered right to your door. Shop their online catalog of over one hundred party themes, personalized gifts, costumes, and supplies for general entertaining. Find Mary Engelbreit's Family & Friends design. First-time customers receive a 10 percent discount when ordering at least $40.00 of merchandise. Click on the animated birthday cake and register all of your family's birthdays and other annual celebrations.

PartyBiz.com will send you an e-mail reminder a week or two before the special day. You will receive occasional updates about new theme parties and upcoming specials.

www.LilBabyCakes.com

You have to check out this Web site if you're looking for a unique baby shower or birthday gift. Lil' Baby Cakes are made of high-quality premium diapers arranged in the shape of a large birthday cake. This is a creative and practical gift for any baby! Each gift is hand assembled and can be shipped directly to the new mother. Lil' Baby Cakes are made of Huggies UltraTrim diapers and they guarantee their product 100 percent. Use this as the centerpiece and check out their party supplies.

www.Partyetc.com

Step right into an index of over eight thousand party items. Categories of Balloons, Tableware, Themes, Weddings, and more are listed to click and browse. Extensive gift wrap and decoration sections make this a must-see site. Cake decorating is another interesting area for those who like to bake their party cakes at home. From food service containers to candles, you should be able to find everything you need for a complete party.

www.AnimalEd.com

Animal Edutainment is a not-for-profit wildlife education outreach organization. Founded in 1990, Animal
Edutainment's facility, based in Texas, is home to over
fifty nonreleasable animals who were orphaned, injured,
surplus, or cast off by previous owners. These animals act
as ambassadors for their species, fostering both children
and adults' curiosity about and respect for the animals
with which we share our world. Click on Party Stuff for
animal-themed party supplies. You can have a Critter-
man Safari Guide party for your grandchildren. Critter-
man is a hands-on program specially designed for
children's parties and family-oriented events.

www.BabyHeirlooms.com

Baby Heirlooms is a mom-and-pop store in Utah.
They've created an electronic catalog of their store. They
carry toys and gifts based on classic children's literature
such as Peter Rabbit, Winnie the Pooh, Madeline,
Paddington Bear, and Curious George. You'll even find
traditional baby clothes (including outfits to wear
home from the hospital) and dress wear for newborns,
infants, and toddlers. Click on Dr. Seuss and you'll find a
wubbulous birthday party idea and supplies. How about
a Curious George celebration? And with the classic
Winnie-the-Pooh characters, you can find a selection
including a first birthday theme.

Kids' TV Shows

Another area for remembering and sharing with your grandchildren can be your childhood character heroes. If you loved that personality or character, more than likely somebody has created a Web site out there with your hero in mind.

If you're a baby boomer grandmother, what was your favorite local children's television show? In the Los Angeles area, we had Sheriff John's Lunch Brigade during the black-and-white era of the late 1950s. I did a search and found some wonderful Web sites for Sheriff John that fans had built over the last couple of years. One site gave me all the lyrics to the famous birthday polka he sang every day. The words to "Put Another Candle on Your Birthday Cake" brought a smile to my face, but what was even better was finding a .wav file (a sound clip) where I could actually hear an old recording of Sheriff John singing the words when I clicked on it. That was a priceless treasure.

Listening to that short clip of music through the computer put me back into the excitement of being a young person myself. I once had the fortune of seeing my hero up close during his personal appearance tour one year. He came to a local shopping center and I was in awe standing in a crowd of children in the cordoned-off parking lot.

Just as we had our heroes, our grandchildren also have theirs. Their television heroes may be Ronald McDonald or Barney, Steve from *Blue's Clues*, or a Disney character. You can help them experience new memories by searching the Internet for sites related to their interests, and then showing them some of yours.

www.Disney.com

You don't have to save money for an expensive trip to Disneyland or Disney World with your grandchildren. At Disney.com you have a magical world of Disney possibilities right on your computer. You have to register, but it's free. Click on Playhouse for a selection of activities for the younger children. Visit Rolie Polie Olie, the magical robot world, and enjoy yourselves with games, activities, music, and stories. Or play with Bear in the Big Blue House. Older grandchildren will want to go into Zeether from the homepage. Click on Games and you have choices of playing games of strategy, sports, or arcade style. Find Disney trivia and contests to enter or shop at the Disney Store.

www.pbs.org

Click on PBS Kids at the Public Broadcasting System homepage. Select one of the characters' names such as Barney, Teletubbies, or Clifford for incredible information regarding the show and its characters. Did you know

Arthur was an aardvark? With Fun and Games, you have a list of over forty different games to play broken out by favorite PBS Kids characters. At Teletubbies, you can play with the Tubby Custard Machine. With Barney, play a dot-to-dot game. Even Mr. Rogers, who finally retired after all these decades, has games for learning and entertainment.

www.SesameWorkshop.org

The Children's Television Workshop brings you the one and only *Sesame Street*. Elmo and friends will provide enjoyment and laughter. Click anywhere on the homepage, Sesame Street takes you to a streetsign corner; you can enter the Kids section or Parents area. Click from the list under Kids, for Games, Art, Music, and Stories. The quality of educational fun you expect from *Sesame Street* is online and available for kids of all ages.

www.CartoonNetwork.com

Cable television has an all-cartoon channel called Cartoon Network. Their Web site is based on the different cartoons. Click on Games from the homepage. You have a variety of choices such as Scooby Doo, the ghost-busting dog and friends, or play with other cartoon characters, such as Quick Draw McGraw, the Jetsons, or the Powerpuff Girls, and their activities. Want More Games will take you into a menu of, what else, more games. That's not all. Click on Toonami for games with the popular

Japanese animation characters such as Sailor Moon and Thunder Cats. The fun never ends.

www.Nick.com

Nickelodeon is a cable television channel filled with kid-sized cartoons and programs. Here at Nick.com you have choices like Games and Music. Click on Games, and scroll down. You can cyber play with different Nick characters, such as Sponge Bob or the kids from Rocket Power, in over fifty games. If that's not enough, you have Brain Games, Sports Games, and Multi-Player games to compete against other Nick.com users. Music gives your grandkids a chance to vote on Snick House Video of the Week or to listen to their favorite Nickelodeon characters on the Nick.com Jukebox. Blab gives the grandchildren a chance to comment on message boards.

www.NickJr.com

Nickelodeon has brought its own special place for preschoolers online. All the different characters the little ones adore are here: Steve and Blue from *Blue's Clues*, Little Bear and friends, Franklin and Little Bill. Even the character Face is here to help you as you make decisions. Click on Games and you can explore activities like learning Spanish with Dora and Tito. Play online with Steve and Blue with weekly activities, as Steve voices encouragement and asks for your help. Click on Stories for animated tales. Click on Art to color online with the cartoon characters. From the homepage, there are also places, including the NickJr store, for grown-ups.

www.FoxKids.com

A favorite television channel for those six and up brings their kids' programs online. *Digimon* and *Power Rangers* are just two of the popular shows you'll find. Click on Games to find choices of Action, Brain, Adventure, and Sports games. Each category gives children an assortment of adventure. Or check out the Top Ten list of favorite games by FoxKids.com users. Click on TV Shows and you can find out more information on the Characters or Frequently Asked Questions. Click on Big Win to check for major contests.

www.WarnerBros.com

From the homepage, you can find out about your favorite television program, movie, or music that Warner Brothers produces. Click on Kids to find a section filled with cartoon character activities. Check out Use Your Brain to find Learn Internet Basics; this is great for any age. Get how-to-use-the-computer tips from your favorite Looney Tunes characters. You can either take one of the quizzes or click on a topic you're interested in learning about. Click on Games from the homepage and you'll find a series of entertainment based on Warner

Brothers projects. The site is set up like a computer network—it's a little cluttered. Just remember that you scroll on the list of games on the left.

Grandma's TV Shows

Hey, we watch television, too. The Internet has a plethora of our own favorite shows highlighting the people we admire, enjoy watching, and/or learning from. Do a search on your favorite television show or celebrity and see what you find. Here are some of my favorites:

www.Oprah.com

This is an excellent site for a variety of reasons. Oprah's staff has created a Web site that will not only tell you what shows are coming up but invites you to e-mail your own story (if it fits into one of the categories of upcoming shows). Click on *The Oprah Show* title, then click Be On The Show for a list of topics such as "Worried about getting old?" or "Did Dr. Phil change your life?" You may be selected to appear on one of her future shows.

www.Rosie.com

Rosie O'Donnell has tremendous positive energy and it comes across on her Web site. Not only can you find out who her guests are going to be for the week, but you'll find celebrity recipes and craft projects under the category

Show Stuff. Click on Rosie's Games and play for prizes such as screen savers for your computer or trading cards in the Rosie's Penny Arcade. Check out the Watch & Win and Rosie's Scratch n' Win Lottery Tickets, which offer a chance to win weekly prizes like Rosie T-shirts and hats.

www.Unsolved.com

Have you ever watched the show *Unsolved Mysteries* and wondered what may have happened after it aired? This Web site is the official site of this program, one of television's first interactive series. Since its premiere, viewers calling the *Unsolved Mysteries* phone center have helped law enforcement officials apprehend approximately 40 percent of the fugitives profiled on the series.

www.ABC.com

This site will bring you close up and personal with information and e-mail access to your favorites stars of ABC television. Find out the latest scoop about *Who Wants To Be A Millionaire* or *The Practice*. Click on ABC Shows and find a quick and easy alphabetical listing of their programs.

www.NBC.com

Find out what's happening with your Must-See TV shows such as *Friends*, *ER*, and *Providence*. Check out the daytime sagas from *Days of Our Lives* and *Passions*; what are the characters involved in now? Use the power of e-mail to give the producers a thought or two you have about their shows.

www.CBS.com

As it says on the homepage, "it's all here." Check out the easy-to-use drop-down menu on the homepage that reads Choose a Show. You'll find access to the prime-time shows such as *Touched by an Angel* and *Everybody Loves Raymond.* Or click on Daytime to find the information and glamour of *The Young and the Restless* or *The Bold and the Beautiful.* To check out something a little heftier, click on *60 Minutes* for the upcoming programs and Program Facts and Bios.

Can you believe all this fun and frivolity is out there on the Internet? Free hours and hours of entertainment, just for us and our grandchildren, be they preschoolers or high school students. Does it get any better than that?

CHAPTER SIX

So Many Hobbies, So Little Time

Being the Grandmothers, the Meemaws, and the Grammys, we should be at a time in our lives where we can immerse ourselves in the things we love most to do—*should* being the operative word in this sentence. In between raising our kids and the laundry and the jobs and the other obstacles on the fast track of life, we've had plenty of time to think about what it is we want to do. Up till now, being the responsible women that we are, what we wanted to do usually took a backseat to what we had to do. With only twenty-four hours in a day, you can do the possible; the impossible takes a little longer. Well, take that time right now and just think about what you like to do for fun, for relaxation, for letting the muse out of the attic where you had her locked away.

Yes, grandchildren can be your favorite hobby. They are the brightest crayons in the box, are they not? Are you an artsy-craftsy kind of grandmother? Share your imagination and your talent with glue with your grandchildren. If you can make a sewing needle do tricks, teach them to the younger generation. And then teach me; my mom tried to share her sewing genes with me and I was all thumbs.

Go to the Internet and explore the world of art, crafts, music, and hobbies—all those wonderful areas we've never had time for or too little time to enjoy. I've listed just a few of the thousands of sites. This is just the tip of the iceberg of imagination and fun.

Kids' Crafts

Are you looking for something to do on a rainy day? Are the grandchildren coming over for the weekend and you have many hours to fill up? There couldn't be a better time for sitting around the kitchen table and working together to make something. The younger ones love making drawings for you to keep on the refrigerator. Are any holidays coming up? Pick one or two projects where the children can make a decoration for your home or theirs.

Even if it is just finger painting, children love to create and design. Help them with a recipe for craft dough, and they can make a handprint cast that, when baked, will last forever. Memories are made, and made special, when you give children an idea and the tools to create it. Find lists of kid-proven projects on the Internet. Pick out a few that are age-appropriate for your sprouting Picassos.

www.about.com

This portal of information can help you find just the right project to work on with your grandkids. Click on Kids. Click on Arts/Crafts for Kids. A main page of projects for kids appears. The list of Subjects on the left gives you a multitude of choices from Papier-Mâché or Origami to Candlemaking or Cartooning. You will find a chat room for Arts/Crafts where you can ask other women about the projects for children or make suggestions of your own.

www.MakingFriends.com

At Making Friends you'll find lots of creative activities for kids ages two through fifteen. They don't get much kid friendlier than here. That's probably because this Web site was researched and developed for the creator's own children, nephews, and nieces. Click on Crafts and find an alphabetical listing of projects, each one rated by age. The table lists Preschool, Elementary, Pre-Teen, and Teen/Adult for easy scanning to find projects for your grandchildren. Each craft comes with a photo of the finished product, a list of materials needed, and easy-to-follow instructions. For convenience, check out their online store for your art supplies.

www.EnchantedLearning.com

Get comfortable, you're going to be here for a while. This is an educational playground. Take any topic and EnchantedLearning.com is going to make it fun for both you and your grandchildren. Before you get overwhelmed with the choices, they have subject pages listed in alphabetical order you can browse through. Or type in a keyword in the search box. I typed in "crafts" and it came up with 260 projects—and that was just the beginning. Enchanted Learning will show you links to additional Web sites for expanding the child's knowledge, with detailed information sheets you can print out.

www.TheIdeaBox.com

Just as the name implies, this Web site is a "box" filled with ideas from people around the world. Click on Activities for an alphabetical index of ideas to keep grandchildren busy for years. Each project gives you a list of materials needed and simple instructions. Click on Games for activities you can play together; instructions on how to play and any materials needed are included with each game. Music and Songs gives you the lyrics to various children's songs that you can sing while working on your arts and crafts.

www.Craftown.com

Craftown.com offers free craft patterns, projects, and tutorials. They have all types of crafts to make or buy—from Country patterns for stenciling and decoupage to Victorian style flower patterns. They have patterns to crochet, knit, sew, and quilt. Click on Kids Crafts. You may want to print out the delightful rules at the beginning, which remind kids to get grown-up help because they like to have fun too. Browse the index of projects. Each craft comes with a "what you need" list and simple "what to do" instructions. Come back often to see what new ideas have arrived.

www.HomeSchoolZone.com

More and more families are opting to school their children at home where they feel they have more control over the quality of the education and the safety of their children. This is a marvelous site for information and projects you can do at home with your grandchildren. Click on the tab Crafts at the top of the page. New crafts, with seasonal themes included, are listed each week. Each project will have a list of materials needed and easy-to-follow instructions.

www.ChildFun.com

Sponsored by WomensForum.com, this is a great site for children's crafts and preschool activities. You can scroll down for a list of ideas on the homepage, or check out the menu of options along the left-hand side. Click on Crafts & Themes for even more project ideas. Sign up to have their weekly crafts report e-mailed to your inbox.

www.NuttinButKids.com

This Web site was originally designed for daycare providers, but grandmothers can also take advantage of the wealth of ideas and projects listed. These are successful activities for the little guys, submitted by the women that know. Scroll down to find a menu of themes to choose from. Choose Ladybugs, Disney, Colors, Babies, and more. With each subject, you'll find songs and play activities, all with learning and having fun in mind.

Crafts to Kids is a subscription program that provides creative, convenient, and inexpensive arts-and-crafts projects to children (ages two to six) and their parents or grandparents. Everything you need to make three fun, educational crafts is included in a packet and mailed to the child or to your home once a month. Each project takes twenty minutes or less to make, depending on how much giggling is involved.

Don't wait around hoping your grandchild will make a holiday present of his or her handprints in clay. Make your own craft dough from recipes at one of the sites above and have your grandchild imprint his or her hand or foot in the clay. Paint them, varnish them, and display them. Do this every year and you'll have a collection to warm your heart when your grandchild has grown and gotten too big to sit at the table and play with Grandma.

Art

If you had a couple hours a week to pamper yourself doing just what your creative heart told you, what would it be? Do you see yourself in a garret writing your memoirs? Are you out in the sun in front of an easel with a palette of paint in your hand? Would you curl up on the couch with a half-finished afghan in your lap, twisting the yarn into a finished product? Now is the time to think of what would be fun to do for you. Remember: Let your creative muse out of the closet and see what magic happens.

www.Craftopia.com

Craftopia.com is one of the foremost craft resources you'll find on the Internet. This site currently claims over sixty thousand products to choose from. Craftopia.com provides you with an easy way to shop for creative supplies. Under each main category, you'll see product information, reviews, expert craft advice and tips, as well as a treasure box of project ideas. Each project comes with a shopping list already made out for you and an estimate of how long the project will take to complete. Enjoy additional features such as an online magazine and mini classes.

www.HobbyPlanet.com

Think of a central station where you will find Internet links to your favorite hobbies. HobbyPlanet.com has done the research for you and put together what it feels are great sites related to subjects you're interested in. Use the Instant Jump to Hobby drop-down menu by clicking on a subject. Or scroll down the homepage and see the categories grouped together for your selection. Click on Crafts to see a menu that includes everything from making scrapbooks to making candles. Each section also includes Frequently Asked Questions, which you'll find very interesting.

www.Art.net

Collections of artists are helping each other share their talents on the World Wide Web. Inside Art.net, artists create and maintain rooms in a gallery where they show their works and share about themselves. Currently this site is international, representing over a hundred artists such as poets, musicians, painters, and sculptors. If you click on Gallery, you'll see virtual hallways to enter by clicking the icons. Or go right to the Gallery Directory and see the list of artists and their rooms. If you've ever thought of having your own show, you could make your dream come true here.

CreativityPortal.searchking.com (no www)

At Creativity Portal, you will have an easy-to-use search engine to techniques and tips about your favorite craft. This started out as someone's personal list of favorite Web sites regarding arts and crafts. Over time it evolved into its own search engine format and opened up to all users on the Internet. Either type in a keyword in the search box or scroll down to look at the Directory. Do you want to learn about Balloon Art? Click on it and you'll see an index of Web sites to help you find the answers to your questions.

www.WorldofWatercolor.com

World of Watercolor is an online magazine for watercolor and acrylic artists and enthusiasts. Art techniques, tips, lessons, and a gallery are some of the features you'll find. Just like a magazine from a newsstand you have Departments, a Current Edition with feature articles, and Special Announcements.

www.ArtCafe.net

This cyber café is filled with artists and muses to help you discover or enhance your own talents. It's an artist community online with features such as ArtPages filled with articles and demonstrations. Learn from experienced artists. Read the tips and tricks, like using any flower vase you have handy to hold your paintbrushes. Enjoy the Artists Message Boards and discuss your concerns and successes with others online.

www.JHPottery.com

John Hester has put together a Web site that includes an excellent seminar for making your own pottery. His Pottery Tutorial is designed for the beginner as a step-by-step guide to making your own ceramics. The first section is designed to give you the most basic techniques and tips. Each section following has illustrations as well as text to explain each step. Because of space requirements, glazing techniques are not yet covered in John's tutorial, but his suggested list of related sites will have examples of how to glaze.

www.AbsoluteWrite.com

If you are interested in freelance writing, screenwriting, playwriting, writing novels, nonfiction, greeting cards, or poetry, you're in the right place. The buttons on the left are categories; click on them to read the table of contents for that particular writer's topic, or click About This Site for a complete map. Scroll down the homepage and check out the Interviews and Articles written by writers for writers. Procrastination, writer's block, and tenacity are all familiar topics. AbsoluteWrite.com is a one-stop Web home for writers of all mediums.

www.Write4Kids.com

Do you have a children's story in your heart that you've toyed with putting down on paper? Here is an excellent Web site on writing for the children's market. Whether you are a beginner, a dreamer, or already published, you will get inspiration and technique from Write4Kids.com. When you ask the question "Where do I get started?" the answer is "Devour this Web site." Tips and info are on every page, under every heading. Warm fuzzies are hidden everywhere. Browse, learn, then sit down and write that story.

Music

When a grandbaby is born into a family, grandfathers may look at the infant's long fingers and see a great ball player. Grandmothers may look at those same sweet dimpled hands and see a magnificent finger spread for playing the piano. If you love and appreciate music, give that same appreciation you have in your heart to your grandchildren. Sit down and show them how Grandma plays the piano or flute. Get them involved in the art of music. See if there is talent in that little package of energy.

www.PianoWorld.com

Piano World is online to help you find any information you want about pianos. There are literally hundreds of pages of facts, figures, fun, and reference material on this Web site. Choose from any of the drop-down menus on the left, or click on the directory link to start exploring. Do you need to find a professional tuner, teacher, mover, or dealer? Do you want to sell your piano? You'll find answers to those questions and also find contests and fun facts, trivia, and music links.

www.Steinway.com

For over a hundred years, Steinway has been dedicated to the ideal of making the finest pianos in the world. Whether you are a professional artist or enthusiastic listener, you will enjoy exploring the rich tradition of these beautiful instruments. A Steinway is the Cadillac of pianos. Categories on the homepage include Technical Info such as how to care for a Steinway and how to find out how old your Steinway may be. You can click on a factory tour where you and your grandchildren can learn about the talent and care that goes into building one of these fine instruments.

www.FluteWorld.com

Flute World, America's flute specialty house, is online to serve you. Easy-to-use drop-down menus under Flute, Piccolo, and Bass Flute will show you a variety of vendors and suppliers. They have a catalog, which includes flute music and chamber music in forty-eight different categories along with a wide variety of flute accessories. All products (sheet music, recorded music, and accessories) except for instruments are purchased through an automated shopping cart system. Instruments are purchased by using a separate secure order form for your convenience. You have a ten-day trial period on any flute you purchase. Be sure to check out their large selection of used instruments.

www.Violink.com

This site is devoted to the world of violins. More than three thousand resources related to stringed instruments all over the world are indexed in easy-to-use categories. This is also a mini search engine for violin enthusiasts. (Think "violin" plus "link" for Violink.com.) From violin makers to concertos, you can browse through the links with new information added regularly.

www.SandboxSymphonyShop.com

With a Web address like that, what else could you expect but fun musical items for your grandchildren? Playful Harmonies, Inc. is the company behind this easy-to-use Web site. Click on any one of the categories to the left and find a detailed description of a variety of items. Click on Tappers and find rhythm sticks and finger cymbals, or check out Scrapers for enameled sand blocks and a Clatterpillar. Easy checkout for online purchases is available.

www.Orchestore.com

What a great place for children's instruments! Based on the Mary Ann Hall's Music for Children program, Orchestore.com has a variety of percussion and handheld kid-sized items. Their instruments have been tested by thousands of children over the past ten years and offer a money-back guarantee. Music kits are available in age-specific ranges. Check out the Chilean rain stick or the glockenspiels.

www.GBase.com

Twenty thousand guitars can't be wrong. This Web site is chock-full of everything you ever wanted to know about guitars. If this site is not for you, maybe it's for the teenaged grandson in your family. You can do a search on thousands of used instruments being sold by hundreds of dealers for the perfect holiday gift. Check out their articles regarding dealers and equipment. You'll find tips galore.

www.MarchingLinks.com

If you're looking for marching band and performing arts–related information on the Web, you've come to the right place. MarchingLinks.com is an index site listing marching band suppliers, designers, publications, events, and units. Are your grandchildren part of the band or tall flags team? Check out this site together. The site does not limit its scope to marching band units as it includes the entire world of tall flags, drum corps, and many other performing groups. Parade rest.

There's nothing that makes a grandmother's heart melt faster than enjoying a Saturday afternoon recital of their grandchild's musical talents—or watching your grandson or granddaughter march in step to the latest half-time extravaganza, even if you have to sit on a hard bench in the freezing cold Friday night air. The shrill notes and thundering beat of the drums stirs the soul, and you want to crush them in a big Nonna hug when they come running up to you afterward with pride and success in their eyes.

Needlecrafts

My mother was a master seamstress, pins down. That woman could look at a piece of clothing and replicate it in her spare time in a variety of fabrics. Her varied-sized granddaughters were outfitted in identical dresses every Christmas. I didn't inherit one sewing gene from this woman. I break out in hives in front of a sewing machine as I watch the needle go up and down. I fix torn hems with Scotch tape. I sew on buttons by purchasing a new shirt. Cross-stitch is me yelling at a piece of thread. Needless to say, needlecrafts are not my thing.

For the rest of you, however, here are Web sites to help you enjoy using your hands to create beauty with a needle.

www.AllStitchedUp.com
This is the world's largest online cross-stitch shop. It has thousands of cross-stitch designs to choose from. To find the design you want, you can search by designer, key-word, or category. The shop also carries fabrics, specialty threads, and tools for cross-stitchery. Discover what cross-stitchers all over the world have discovered: This is

the easiest way to shop for cross-stitch supplies. Materials for other types of needle arts are also available. Choose from latch hook, embroidery (including crewel), or plastic canvas.

www.Auntie.com

Like your favorite auntie, this site is warm, friendly, and a must-see experience. Auntie.com has put together links to creative Web sites and informational pages on dolls, crafts, and miscellaneous fun like a cookbook, contests, and e-mail groups. The Quilting section sends you into quality areas of helpfulness like The Quilt Mall or Buy the Bolt Web site. Check out Auntie's Paper-Dolls.com and find treasures to order through association with Amazon.com. Don't forget to check out Auntie's Favorite Links to find new and exciting places of adventure online.

www.Crochet.org

This is the official Web site of the Crochet Guild of America, a nonprofit organization that wants to preserve the craft and quality of the art of crocheting. Check out the section on news and conferences, then scroll down the homepage to Crochet Resources. You'll find How To Crochet Lessons, with separate instructions for left and right-handers. Easy step-by-step directions with graphics will help you and your grandchildren work together. Join or set up a local chapter in your community. Meetings are an opportunity for showing works in progress, as well as for sharing information about local yarn and supply sources.

www.joann.com

Jo-Ann Fabrics & Crafts is online with all the quality and customer service you've enjoyed at their stores for years. Be sure to become a member—it's free—so you can take part in all their Community page options, like chat rooms, message boards, and the wish list. You will be able to sell your crafts in the Street Fair. Once you're a member, shopping will be even more convenient as they will fill in part of your order form automatically, remember the items in your past shopping carts, keep all of your shipping addresses on file, and track all of your orders.

www.Craftopia.com

Craftopia.com is one of the foremost needlecraft resources. It provides you with an easy way to shop for thread, needles, yarn, patterns, and more. Under main categories, such as Fabric & Trim or Needle Crafts, you'll see product information, reviews, expert craft advice and tips as well as a treasure chest of project ideas. Each project comes with a shopping list for supplies and an estimate of how long the project will take to complete. Enjoy additional features such as an online magazine and mini classes.

www.HickoryHillQuilts.com

Check out this easy-to-use online catalog. Hickory-
HillQuilts.com offers a wide variety of items for the
antique quilt enthusiast and quilters interested in
restoration or reproduction of quilts. In addition to a selection of antique quilts and quilt tops, they also carry new
quilt fabric, patterns, batting, and quilt heritage books.

www.QuiltBus.com

Just like it sounds, the Quilt Bus is a quilt store that
comes to your door with fabrics, patterns, kits, books,
and ideas. Visit the QuiltBus online for quilt patterns,
fabric kits, quilting and sewing supplies, paper-pieced
patterns, free quilt block patterns, and quilt books. Find
EQ4 tips (Electric Quilt, a computer program for
designing quilts) and quilting tips, terms and tutorials,
patchwork information, links, block of the month, and
mystery quilts.

RUBBER STAMPS

My rubber stamp collection is housed in an antique medical form cabinet made out of oak I found at a yard sale.
Each of the eighteen drawers is ten by fifteen inches and
only an inch deep, perfect for housing the hundreds of
stamps I own. Each drawer holds a different category

and I use them on envelopes and stationery, though my efforts are nothing compared with those of the rubber stamp enthusiasts I've met. I bow to their talents for homemade invitations and holiday cards.

My grandsons do not share my enjoyment of stamping. A few stamps here and there on a blank piece of paper and they're ready to move on to something more fun. However, get out a pad of washable ink and they'll stamp the back of their arms, hands, and each other's faces and not blink an eye.

Here are two sites to keep you, as well as granddaughters and grandsons, happily stamping:

www.Stamparoo.com

Here is a great online rubber stamps catalog. Stamparoo.com offers thousands of individual decorative rubber stamps for you to choose from in their Rubber Stamp Gallery. Categories are divided by subject and by the names of renowned stamp artists. Click on Flavia for her sketchings or Joy Marie with her pansies and daisies. Each stamp comes with a viewable image (click on it for a larger viewing), and you can buy the rubber stamps online with the secure and easy-to-use checkout. Don't forget to click on stamping and embossing accessories.

Canning and Pickling

Canning is a tradition that can save you money and be a very rewarding hobby for you and your grandchildren. Most grandkids think vegetables come from the grocery store in a can or frozen in a plastic bag. Help them experience the satisfaction of completing a jar of jam or pickle relish. They'll probably want to eat it the next day—patience is not always a virtue with them—but the memories of making the delicious recipes will linger forever in your heart.

I recommend doing a search at one of your favorite search engines, such as Yahoo.com or Google.com, and use "home canning" as your keywords. Many of the canning sites and recipes are buried in URL addresses that would cramp the heartiest typist by entering them. You don't want to miss out on the rich resources available on the Internet. Here are just a few I found that had easy-to-remember addresses.

www.homecanning.com

One of the simple joys that dates back generations is home canning. This site has a terrific Basic Guideline that will take you step-by-step through the process, explaining as you go the whys and hows along the way. You can click on Equipment for an easy list of each item you can use. Ball jars and Kerr products are recommended. Click on Recipes and browse their recipe categories or use the handy keyword search to find the recipes you're looking for. To view all recipes within a category, select a category from the drop-down menu and click Find It.

www.GBICanning.com

From the company that has provided room-decorating solutions in that beautiful glass block, GBI now introduces GBI Canning online. Click on Product Line, then Canning. Check out their round-rim jars. The mouth of this patented jar is designed to give an extremely secure and firm seal on the processed and cooled jars. Not only do they look great, they're stackable. Then go to the Tulip jars, Deco, and the Mold jars. Click on Canners for their line of electric canners that can be used anywhere.

homecanningsupply.com (no www)

Here is an online catalog with pages of canning equipment, canning supplies, canning tools, canning books, dehydrators, pressure canners, steam canners, steamer juicers, food strainers, meat grinders, and grain grinders—something for everything. You cannot order these items online however. Their catalog can be sent to you by snail mail, or call their 800 number to order products.

www.Mountain-Breeze.com

The Coldiron family of Kentucky is busy with both Web designing and working in the kitchen. Click on The Kitchen and then click on Canning Recipes for some of their own family concoctions that will make your mouth water. Check out the recipe for Sweet Potatoes, a candied concoction, or make your own sauerkraut in a jar. There are some additional canning recipes under Down Home Cooking and the Melton Family. Be sure to check those out.

www.ilovepickles.org

Peter Piper never had it so good. Click on Pickled Particulars for articles on Cooking Tips, Crazy Facts, Snacking, and Entertaining. Pickles, pickled peppers, and sauerkraut are what this site is all about. Click on Shopping to go to the Pickle Store. "For those with a passion for pickles, we offer a number of particularly pleasing pieces of pickle paraphernalia," say the people from the Pickle Packers International, Inc., a trade association for the pickled vegetable industry. You have to check out the pickle-chip earrings. You can wear these while pickling with the grandkids. And they're perfect for any family picnic.

www.Picklenet.com

On this site you will find useful information to get you started in the wonderful world of pickling. Click on The Basics to find out what ingredients you'll need, what equipment to use, and how to sterilize containers. Picklenet.com has tons of tasty pickle and chutney recipes, even flavored vinegar. You'll find links to online pickle shops, such as Pettigrews of Kelso in Scotland. Get expert advice from—whom else—their resident pickle expert, Pete.

www.PickleKing.com

Yes, there is a self-appointed pickle king: Rob Fleischer. Welcome to his Pickle Preservation Society. If you can get past the green type on black background, Rob does have a recipe section for pickled items sent to him from people everywhere. He's divided them into four categories where you'll find mouthwatering taste treats.

Gardening

When it comes to growing anything besides animals and children, I have a brown thumb. Okay, I admit it. My total exposure to horticulture was a sweet potato vine project when I was ten years old, and an avocado seed that sprouted when I was about twenty-four. For me, food came from stores, and flowers came from florists. My parents were both raised on farms, but they never turned a shovel of dirt again after they left the farm. Hence, I lived the city life and raised my next generation the same way.

Then along comes a grandson and I get this wild idea to grow our own pumpkins for Halloween. Hey, it could happen. Out of the sandy Southern California soil, we dug little mounds of earth and planted seeds. Nowhere in the tiny print on the back of the seed package directions did it say not to have the sprinkler running every day. Despite my ineptitude, we did manage to get a whopping two tiny pumpkins the first year. Nothing the second.

I sat down at the computer and went to the Internet to ask what I was doing wrong. I found Web sites on pumpkins that answered the hows and what-to-dos in growing a decent-sized jack-o'-lantern type pumpkin. Pollination, snipping, and fertilizing became buzz words for our next crop.

For all you Earth Goddesses, those that love to get their hands dirty with Mother Nature, there are excellent gardening sites available. I live more by this slogan: "By the time you find greener pastures, you can't climb over the fence." The rest of you go and plant your hearts out.

www.Garden.org

Note that this site is a "dot-org" or organization. It's the site of the National Gardening Association, which for the last two decades has been helping gardeners and helping people through gardening. Under Gardening Resources, you'll be able to do a search by keywords through their articles on gardening or through Questions and Answers for specific information. Click on How-To for a menu of project areas such as Patio Gardening, Roses, or Vegetable Gardening. Each project is broken down into a list of topics that includes what tools are needed and handy tips. Check out Garden.org's Community for their Events Calendar. You can do a search of your area for upcoming plant sales, festivals, or exhibits. Enjoy yourself on the Message Boards where you can communicate with other gardeners under specific headings such as Flowering Plants or Seed Starting.

www.GardenWeb.com

Think of a garden community and you have Garden-
Web. Here you will find a variety of forums for discussion on everything from roses to regional plant life.
Browse through the index of subject titles to find those
of interest to you. Check out Exchanges & Trading. In a
forum environment, you can find what other gardeners
are offering for sale or trade, in seeds and plants or post
your own offerings.

www.NoProblemGarden.com

Sit back and relax while you read the Garden Diary of
Lindley Karstens. Her down-to-earth experiences will
mimic quite a few of our own. Click on Common Fixes
for fixes to everyday problems when tilling the soil. From
Hot And Dry Areas to Soggy Places, you can find many
gardening answers. If not, Lindley has set up a menu of
gardening links you can jump to for more intricate information.

www.OrganicGardening.com

Organic gardening does not involve the use of synthetic
fertilizers or pesticides on plants. OrganicGardening.com
says to begin with attention to the soil by regularly adding
organic matter to it. Grass clippings, fall leaves, and vegetable scraps from your kitchen are the building blocks of
compost, the ideal organic matter for your garden soil. If

you add compost to your soil, you're already well on your way to raising a beautiful, healthy garden. If after OG Basics you still have problems with your organic garden, check out Solutions Online.

www.WindowBox.com

WindowBox.com has all the information and supplies you need to grow flowers, vegetables, and herbs on your porch, deck, terrace, patio, or windowsill. You find a place, they can help you grow something there. They sell exclusive products and a vast selection of gardening containers. If you are not completely satisfied, you can return any item for replacement, full reimbursement, or store credit for 112 percent of the value.

www.WaysideGardens.com

Wayside Gardens, one of the most respected mail-order nurseries in the United States, is online. Here is a premier source of choice plants and bulbs with exciting, never-before-seen introductions, rare heirlooms, and classic favorites. Products are divided into ten categories from Trees to Edibles. Each section has an alphabetical listing of plants, plus helpful segments on shade, sun, and partial sun preferences. Enjoy garden tips and sign up for their newsletters. Be sure to check their Web Specials often.

www.DaydreamerGardens.com

For sale online, Daydreamer Aquatic Gardens carries aquatic and pond plants including water lilies, lotus, marginals, and bog. You'll also find land plants for your home. Check out their convenient Catalog Search. You can search for a plant based on characteristics that include (but are not limited to) bloom color or bloom period for a plant. Click on Planting Instructions for tips and tricks in growing hardy lilies or starting a perennial border. Learn to grow and maintain tropical lilies.

www.kidsgardening.com

The National Garden Association (NGA) brings you a fun and informational site for getting your grandchildren involved and excited about gardening. Click on the Parent's Primer for techniques and garden projects to do with the grandchildren. See how to design and build a kids' garden, prepare soil, and plant with age-specific tips. The NGA wants you to take advantage of gardening moments with your grandkids every chance you can in your own backyard, in the garage, or at the windowsill. Click on the KidsGardening Store for fun and useful items, such as a flower press kit or sun print-making kit.

Volunteering

When I was a little girl, I wanted to be a guide dog trainer more than anything else in the world. Guide dogs are the western United States' equivalent to Seeing Eye dogs and Leader dogs, wonderful creatures that help guide a blind person to a more independent lifestyle. Guess what? It was a male-only field back in the early 1960s, and I was furious and bitter over the rejection. I still have the no-thank-you letter from the school where I sought employment.

Flash forward to the 1990s and I discovered that Guide Dogs of the Desert (GDD) in Palm Desert, California, took local volunteers for their Adult Puppy Raising Program. After filling out the forms and waiting for a litter to be available, I finally became a puppy raiser for this adorable yellow lab pup named Oscar. He was mine for a year to socialize and train in a variety of ways, including taking him into grocery stores wearing a fabric jacket identifying him as a service dog in training. This was the beginning of years of volunteer involvement with GDD.

After Oscar came Bayou and Harmony. Imagine the heartfelt tears at the graduation ceremony when I escorted Harmony to a stage where her new owner was waiting for her. By volunteering, a dream came true for me. I was a part of the miracle in working with these gallant dogs and the visually impaired.

Grandma ONLINE

Nothing compares to the feeling of doing something for someone else. Volunteering gives us the opportunity to help those less fortunate, better our community, and strengthen our future generations. Use the Internet to find organizations that need your skills and that want your support and energy. It'll brighten your day and that of so many others.

www.usaweekend.com/diffday

Make A Difference Day, the largest national day of helping others, is sponsored by *USA Weekend* magazine and its over 560 carrier newspapers nationwide. The fourth Saturday of October has become synonymous with volunteering your time and effort to help others. Anyone and everyone can participate. Do you want to help but don't know what to do? Click on Idea Generator and answer the three questions. Then click on Give Me Ideas and you will see a list of projects and concepts to choose from.

www.LiteracyVolunteers.org

Become a Literacy Volunteers of America (LVA) volunteer and you will have the power to change the lives of adults in your community by helping them learn to read. LVA has affiliates in over forty states. Find your state on their map to find an affiliate in your community. If you cannot find a local LVA affiliate, please check your local Yellow Pages for the literacy program nearest you.

www.PTA.org

The National PTA needs volunteer help now more than ever. Get involved in your grandchild's school. If your grandchildren live out of state, volunteer at your local schools and give as many hours of energy as you can. Budget cuts have hurt our nation's schools, and it is the strength and support of volunteers that elevate the quality of education for our grandchildren. Check out this site for valuable information on what is happening with the PTA and where you can join.

www.PedAIDS.org

The Elizabeth Glaser Pediatric AIDS Foundation needs volunteers living in the Santa Monica, California, area to assist with general office duties during regular office hours and with occasional weekend projects, such as mailings and events. Through the generosity of dedicated volunteers, the foundation maintains a less than 6 percent administrative overhead. If you don't live in Southern California, you can still participate. Click on How You Can Help from the homepage to see a list of ideas and suggestions for helping to support this wonderful organization. Research money is desperately needed to help children infected with HIV.

www.FamilyCares.org

Welcome to Family Cares, an online resource that empowers families to make a difference in their communities. Membership is free. Their goal is to help you promote compassion and the spirit of charity in children through hands-on family projects that help others in need. As a part of this, grandmothers can help teach the grandkids to be good Samaritans, to learn an attitude of gratitude, and to understand that charity begins at home, wherever home may be.

www.HSUS.org

The Humane Society of the United States wants your help. To learn about volunteer opportunities with animal protection organizations in your community, HSUS.org suggests you check your Yellow Pages under the headings "animal shelter," "humane society," and "animal control," or call Information. You will need to contact each group directly to learn about their particular volunteer needs and opportunities. Click on Frequently Asked Questions for more information. Click on For Kids and Teens from the homepage to find education and entertainment options for the younger generation in learning about animal protection and preserving nature. Scroll down for an index of choices.

www.DogsfortheDeaf.org

Dogs for the Deaf, Inc., in Oregon is a nonprofit organization that provides four-footed hearing companions to the hearing impaired. Hearing Dogs are chosen from animal shelters, where they might otherwise be euthanized if no homes are found for them. By using shelter dogs, Dogs for the Deaf is able to help alleviate some of the unwanted dog population by rescuing these dogs, professionally training them, and placing them in loving homes where they can provide an important service.

www.CanineCompanions.org

Canine Companions for Independence (CCI) is a school that produces remarkable animals that provide assistance to people with disabilities. The dogs are trained to respond to over a hundred commands to make the lives of their owners easier and more independent. Click on How Can You Help? to find out about volunteer opportunities and contributions needed. One of the most helpful things you can do is share the idea of CCI with others. If you are aware of family, friends, clubs, or organizations that might be interested in CCI's services or interested in volunteer opportunities, share the knowledge you'll find on this Web site and direct them to CanineCompanions.org.

Dr. Norman Vincent Peale founded Guideposts in 1945 as a way to help people from all walks of life achieve their maximum personal and spiritual potential. Click on Help Us Help Others. Guideposts lists several different ways for you to contribute to help others less fortunate, such as the Sweater Project. The Guideposts Sweater Project collected over sixty thousand children's sweaters in a three-year period. All of these sweaters are hand-knit (or crocheted) by volunteers like yourself who donate their skills, time, materials, and the postage to get them to Guideposts. If you are interested in creating baby and children's sweaters for little ones around the world, please send your sweaters to: Guideposts Sweater Project, c/o Brigitte Weeks, 16 East 34th Street, New York, NY 10016.

Dancing

How many of us remember slipping into our tap shoes at a tender age in hopes of being the next Shirley Temple, or joining a crooked line of tots concentrating on learning "Shuffle Off to Buffalo." Even though colored leotards did nothing for our little potbellies of baby fat, we didn't mind standing in front of a huge mirror under harsh glaring lights back then. (Now, of course, it's a different story: We break into a sweat whenever we find ourselves facing a mirror inside a fitting room.)

During the last two years of high school, and a little beyond, I was very involved in Polynesian dancing with Miss Betty's tutorage out of her Chino studio. I owned two grass skirts from Tahiti and my own feather gourds, which were part of the outfit I wore as our Polynesian dance troupe performed off and on all summer. It had been a dream of my mother's to take a trip to the Hawaiian Islands. These dance classes and local luau performances were as close as she got.

I hung up my leis long ago, but I still enjoy dancing. I've taken a few classes of ballroom dancing with the local recreation department. And guess what? You can find line dancing, two stepping, belly dancing, or Lindy Hop information on the Internet. It's not as much fun to read about it as it is to do it, but these sites might give you the incentive to sign up for instruction.

www.dosado.com

Here is an Internet portal to Western square dancing. Though much of the dance can be traced back to French or English roots, we think of square dancing as an American institution of entertainment. Yee-haw! You can click on Articles for information regarding the history of square dancing, classes, or advice. Click on Callers Corner for Web sites regarding definitions of dance steps and resources. The index includes choreography, callers listings, and callers wanted.

www.offjazz.com

Click on Jazz + Tap Dance to find an index of choices regarding both of these dances. You can click on Terminology for tap and find the step definitions for shuffle, stomp, and brush-and-ball change. If you have patience to wait for the downloading of video clip files, there are some excellent pieces to show you the steps and how they are performed. Click on the video for the Time Step and you see a pair of feet dancing off the rhythm. From the Jazz & Tap page, click on Tap Dance and you'll see the basic steps. Keep scrolling down and there are video clips of the professional dancers we love: Bill Robinson, Fred Astaire, and Gene Kelly.

www.Shira.net

The Art of Middle Eastern Dance by Shira is an oasis for belly dancers that offers belly dancing education, inspiration, and entertainment. One of the great things about Oriental dance is that you can do it regardless of your age or figure type. The dance moves complement the way a normal human body moves. You'll find hundreds of articles, cartoons, and opinion polls—all related to belly dancing.

www.dancescape.com

If you love ballroom competition dancing, this is a site for you. Dancescape.com is one of the world's leading online magazine and information sites about ballroom dancing as a sport. Ballroom competitions gained popularity during the early 1920s. Read about how the International Olympic Committee has recognized Dance Sport as a legitimate sport, and how DanceSport competitors would like to one day compete in the Olympics. Click on Media Highlights and find short clips of dancing e-greetings you can send to your friends.

www.AnySwingGoes.com

For those of you that love dancing to the big band sound, here is a free online magazine devoted to the revival of swing and big band music and dancing. Check out their comprehensive links directory, contests, news, and band information. Click on Swing MP3s to hear clips of songs we remember. Click on Latest News to read about what's happening where in the big band arena.

www.ScottishDance.net

Grand Chain is a set of resources for Scottish dancers or lovers of the dance the world over. Based in Edinburgh, this online center offers information on Scottish Country Dance, Ceilidh, Highland, Step, and Reeling. Click on Ceilidh Dances and you'll have written instructions on the specific dance steps to a variety of songs. Click on Hints and Tips for dance etiquette and how to dress.

www.LineDanceFun.com

Do you understand that a 32-count, 2-wall, no-tag dance can be done to any slow nightclub two-step music? If you do, this site is for you. Though this site is mainly a Southern Californian event scheduler of country-western dance happenings, you can scroll down to the last third of the site for dance sheets and music clips of country-western music. Tush-Push is listed under Request List Oldies.

www.DancinUpaStorm.com

Dancin Up a Storm is the official Web site of country-western DJ Karen Hedges. You can click on her Biography or spend time in the Chat Room talking with other two-steppers. Click on Choreography for line dance steps to a list of titles. Check out the Online Store for Karen's own Dancin Up A Storm clothing items.

Our spare time is a way to relax and enjoy ourselves, whether we do it sitting down or twirling around the dance floor. Whether we're up to our elbows in compost or knotting the thread of a masterpiece, we've earned this respite into pleasure. Take your grandchildren under your wing and share the experience with them. Give them the desire to create and think outside the ordinary routines. Help them discover the thrill of completion after hours—or well, at least twenty minutes, which to preschoolers is the same thing—of concentration. When grandma's happy, everyone is happy.

Are We There Yet?

As parents, we looked on vacation trips with our kids as something more like torture than travel. We made the annual trek to somewhere they didn't want to go, and the "he's looking at me, she's on my side" complaints continued mile after mile. It's not to say that traveling with the grandchildren is any easier. They are still kids after all and usually do not like to be cooped up in small spaces for long. Maybe it is the fact that we have a choice whether they come with us or not that gives us a deeper patience with their youthful exasperations.

Driving in any kind of car today limits each child and grandparent to the area of his or her seat belt. An identical situation occurs if you are flying together, except you have less personal space. You have to be creative in the entertainment department due to the controlled and cramped environment.

Whether you're traveling to go see the grandkids or taking them with you somewhere on vacation, the Internet can be a handy, dandy helper. You have services at your fingertips that you used to have to run all over town to use. From the comfort of home you can make plane or train reservations, print a map of the exact location you're going to, and you can check on the weather of your destination anytime, day or night. Again, the Internet is open twenty-four hours a day, seven days a week. If you are worried about an approaching storm during your trip to Kansas, don't worry about clicking your ruby slippers

Grandma ONLINE

together three times. You check out the five-day weather forecast in the middle of the night and assuage those fears—or make alternate plans if necessary.

Let me add a serious note, if I may. If you are going to be traveling with your grandchildren without their parents along (and trips are a wonderful time for bonding), be sure to have the parent(s) sign an emergency medical slip for you to keep in your purse just in case. Should anything happen during your travels, this release form gives you permission to get medical and hospital help for the child. It is better to have it with you and not need it than to be in need of urgent medical care and spend precious time trying to call the parents from the emergency room.

That said, let's go look on the Internet for travel information. We can look into all-inclusive vacation packages for an extensive adventure with your grandchildren, cruises on the high seas, or explorations in national forests and parks. The Internet becomes an electronic travel agent just for you.

Travel and Vacation

During school vacation excursions with your grandkids, you can take them to Disney World or Epcot Center in Florida, spend a weekend at the Grand Canyon, or enjoy the Southern California amusement park tour from

Knott's Berry Farm to Sea World. What happens after that? Use the Internet to find something a little different in traveling ideas for next year. You are only limited by your imagination.

www.Travel.com

A quick and easy way to start any travel strategy is at Travel.com. It's like a search engine just for travel. From the main page you can select from a variety of topics related to vacations and excursions. What about sports? Would you like to take the grandkids on a baseball stadium marathon, or how about finding information about the sports departments of different universities for your teenaged grandchildren? There are over fifty thousand links to sports sites alone from this one Web site—and what an easy name to remember, Travel.com.

www.4anything.com

Click on Travel & Local. This is another good source with multiple sections broken out for ease of research. You can spend many hours researching wonderful places around the country and around the globe to visit. Dream and plan to your heart's content.

www.ClubMed.com

Club Med is an international travel and vacation service. Check out which of these all-inclusive resorts have facilities for grandchildren. They list their Baby Clubs, for children four months to twenty-three months old; Petit Clubs for two- and three-year-olds; or Mini Clubs for four- to twelve-year-olds. Let their excellently trained staff help you entertain and delight the little ones while you enjoy Club Med's extensive list of adult activities or dine on delicious buffets.

www.SuperClubs.com

Super Clubs means hassle-free, all-inclusive Caribbean holidays with no hidden costs. SuperClubs.com has nine active resorts with more in planning and development stages. Their Super-Inclusive holidays consist of accommodations; all meals plus snacks and premium brand cocktails; use of all land and water-sports facilities, with equipment and instruction; entertainment; recreational activities; hotel taxes; and airport transfers. Check out FAQ (Frequently Asked Questions) for more detailed information.

www.Sunfinder.com

The staff at Sunfinder.com has visited and researched each of the destinations featured on this Web site providing you with useful, unbiased information to help you plan and book a great vacation. Check out the headings on the left. You can click on specific vacation areas like the Bahamas or Mexico. Or go directly to Choose Your Destination.

Sunfinder.com works with leading wholesalers to provide vacation packages that offer quality and value.

www.Coastal-Travel.com

Travel By Design, a division of Coastal Travel, has set up this Web site to help you plan the perfect vacation, whether you're thinking of an all-inclusive package or of relaxing at a spa and golf location. Check out the Hot Deals section, or click on Family Vacations for prices and destinations. Online registration is available for your convenience. Once you book a trip, you can access Sabre's Virtually There. This Web site gives you up-to-the-minute itinerary and destination information all personalized just for your vacation plans.

www.6-star.com

We all know the term five-star hotel. The people behind 6-star.com believe they are taking the concept one step further with their resorts in and around Cancun, Mexico. All-inclusive vacation packages from Palace Resorts can include day excursions, massages, manicures, and many other amenities, as well as beautiful rooms with ocean views. Click on any of the six Palace names for detailed information for each location.

www.EscapetoEden.com

This travel agency is dedicated to providing you with service and the lowest available rates on a variety of all-inclusive vacations or Las Vegas packages. Click on Las Vegas and find a menu of resorts and hotels with categories that rate accommodations, such as Grand Deluxe to Standard/Superior. Click on one of the hot spots listed off the homepage for detailed information on Caribbean vacations. Price quotes are provided through e-mail, or call their 800 numbers.

www.ClubHolidays.com

Want to compare the various all-inclusive resorts? Think of this site as a virtual vacation brochure. At ClubHolidays.com, they deal with all the big names: Club Med, Super Clubs, the list goes on. Whether you're traveling alone, as a couple, or as a family, let them expertly answer questions as to why you might chose one location or service over another.

www.TahoeDixie2.com

Want to spend a cozy weekend at Lake Tahoe? Zephyr Cove Resort has a winter package built around a three-night stay in lakeside cabins, just steps from the water's edge. Also included is an Emerald Bay sightseeing cruise for two aboard the M.S. Dixie II Paddlewheel. From the Zephyr Cove Snowmobile Center you'll wind through forests on snowmobiles and crest the ridgeline at nearly 9,000 feet for spectacular views of Lake Tahoe. Some meals included. If winter sounds too chilly, try one of their spring vacations.

Travel.org (no www)
As a travel directory, this site opens the world for you. Click on any of the twelve globes for informational Web sites regarding traveling to other countries or continents, or right here in your own backyard. One globe is Lodging, one is for Airlines. Others include Latin America and the South Pacific. Just choose the information you're looking for in vacation travel.

www.Our-Dream-Vacation.com
With a name like that, what else would you find but dreamy vacation plans? Scroll down the page and some favorite vacation spots are listed for your convenience. Click on Europe or England, Mexico or Jamaica to find easy-to-read tables showing various details, such as how many nights in the vacation package. Check out the Description to see if airfare is included. This site also has a section called Vacation Tools. Click here to find a Currency Converter, World Time, World Weather, and Average Temp features.

www.OnlineVacationMall.com

The Online Vacation Mall offers flexibility and choices for the "do-it-yourselfer" to create the ideal vacation. You'll be able to set up your own reservations including air travel, hotel accommodations, car rentals, attraction tickets, and more. Create and buy your own complete vacations to the most popular destinations and find bulk vacation pricing directly from the most trusted brand names in the travel industry. The Online Vacation Mall enables you to plan, price, and buy their vacation deals, all in one secure location.

MAP WEB SITES

You know how most men wouldn't be caught dead asking for directions to get somewhere; thank goodness, we do not suffer from the same communication block. This is your opportunity to find out where you're going and how to get there by using the Internet. Knowledge is a wonderful security blanket. There are various sites on the Internet where you can type in an address anywhere in the United States and it will automatically bring up a small map of that area. You can zoom out to make the map cover more square miles and find out exactly which highways or freeways to use to get there. You can print out the maps.

Never rely on a man's sense of direction again. Check out the location and how to get there for yourself at one of these sites:

www.MapQuest.com

Find out how to get from your door to the point of destination. Each turn or change of road is listed on a separated line. It tells you how many miles you'll be on a certain street or freeway. It also gives you an estimated time of the trip.

www.MapBlast.com

This is fairly simple to use. Type in an address or location, and Mapblast.com will bring up a detailed street map. Click on Zoom In and Zoom Out to get more or less detail on streets and cross streets, as you need them.

www.MapsOnUs.com

You can register for free and they will save your destination addresses for you. They also have a plan-a-route section that tells you exactly how to go from one address to another and approximately how long it will take to get there.

www.Interstate4U.com

This has much more than just maps and directions. It offers a list of travel games to play under When Will We

Be There? and a quick guide to state park information. Just click on the state of your choice for vacation ideas or suggestions. You can also click on Hotels, Restaurants, and Attractions.

Maps.Yahoo.com

Get customized maps and driving directions from Yahoo. Just type in an address and click on Get Map. Use the Zoom In and Zoom Out features to find just what you're looking for. If you need door-to-door directions, click on Driving Directions and type in where you are and where you're going. It's that simple.

Once you're on the road, depending on their age, let your grandchildren hold the directions and check off each turn as you go along. It will make them feel important to be the navigator and give them more of an understanding how long the trip will take.

Online Tickets

Moving out of state and away from the grandchildren has made me a frequent flyer. I wanted to take a trip during the Mother's Day weekend to visit my grandsons. What better Mother's Day gift to myself than to get sticky hugs and squeals of laughter on that special Sunday morning.

I went out to the Net and found available flight information. Within minutes, I knew what the prices were going to be. I made my reservations and received my confirmation number all online, with a round-trip schedule that would work for all involved. It was the greatest gift to myself.

No need to wait for a holiday to make a journey. You have the power of being a travel agent right at your fingertips, even if you're in your robe and slippers. You can see the different airlines to compare time schedules and prices, and can make appropriate choices.

www.biztravel.com

This airline reservation site requests a personal profile from the beginning or you may enter as a guest. Click on Travel Planner to start a new reservation. One nice feature is Repeat a Trip, if you mainly fly to one destination. Using biztravel.com site, you can track and manage multiple frequent travel programs through its bizmiles service. You have access to experienced travel professionals twenty-four hours a day, seven days a week, either online or via a toll-free number.

www.Expedia.com

Whether looking for flights, lodging, car rentals, or any combination, you have more choices and increased savings on travel with Expedia.com. This travel Web site will help you with most of your vacation needs. Click on Flights to set up airline tickets. Expedia.com will show you the least expensive or those closest matching your schedule, without cluttering you with every flight available. You can request a specific seat using their featured Seat Pinpointer. Click on Hotels for lodging. Use the Hotel Wizard to quickly set up an advanced search for your needs. Or click on Packages and see if you can save money by booking a flight and hotel room at the same time.

www.Travelocity.com

Travelocity.com is one of the most useful one-stop travel sites on the Internet providing secure online reservation capabilities for air, car, hotel, and vacation reservations. You also have access here to a vast database of destination and other travel information. Use the feature Best Fare Finder to find the lowest airfare to where you want to go. While booking your flight, you can select specific seats with online seat maps. Use Vacation Finder for quick information about possible vacation and cruise packages.

www.Travelscape.com

Travelscape.com is a complete do-it-yourself travel site on the Internet. Travelscape.com has a "10 clicks or less" guarantee that it will outperform any other online travel site in providing you the quickest, easiest, and most convenient way to book air, lodging, and auto rental package to the top destinations in the nation. Don't just use the Reservation features. Check out their Specials and Hot Deals.

www.Lowestfare.com

Lowestfare.com is a full-service Web site of discount travel products and services. They sell discounted tickets and published fares on all major airlines and provide reservations for hotels, car rentals, and discounted cruise and tour packages. Heavy discounts are available from twelve major cities in the United States. Check out their Hot Vacation Deals and Florida Packages.

www.AirfareStore.com

This is a newer, smaller site that is building a reputation for searching for domestic and international discount air-fares. Once you give them the criteria of your departure and destination cities and dates, it will list out available airlines and prices. Online reservation service is not available on this site. After you have completed your search, you will be given the option to have a copy of selected fares and additional information e-mailed to you. Included in the e-mail will be information on how to purchase tickets.

www.aa.com

American Airlines is ready to help you schedule your airfare online. Become a member of one of the most popular frequent-flyer programs in the world. You'll get complete access to this site, letting you book flights online, manage your AAdvantage account, and discover AAdvantage special offers. Best of all, membership is free. Want to check on an incoming American flight? Click on Travel Planning, then click on Check Flight Status. Type in the flight number and day of arrival for online information to see arrival status.

www.ual.com

Flying the friendly skies with United Airlines just got friendlier. Easy to use, this Web site allows you to check a flight status or find a quick fare right from the homepage. Be sure to check out the E-fares that are special discounted airfares priced to go. United has provided a list of Travel Services for your convenience as well. Click on Baggage to have questions answered about quantity and size of luggage, or special pieces. Are you a Mileage Plus member? Check out the status of your account online any time.

www.Amtrak.com

With free registration, you can purchase Amtrak railway tickets online from their official Web site. Browse their schedules and fares. Check out the Rail Sale area for exclusive online discounted travel. These discounts apply not just to travel between the two cities listed, but all Amtrak stops in between. Prices and dates available are listed. Click on Special Offers from the homepage for additional savings and vacation packages. If you're traveling with your grandchildren by train, click on Fun & Games and check out the Amtrak Store. You can buy Amtrak T-shirts and backpacks to make traveling by train even more memorable.

www.Greyhound.com

Greyhound Lines, the largest national intercity bus service, has its own Web page. You can purchase tickets online. They will be sent to you by first class mail, so they must be ordered at least ten days ahead of the departure date to ensure delivery. Greyhound offers an Ameripass, which is good for up to sixty days of consecutive travel anywhere. Destinations and route maps are available on this site.

Bargain Traveling

Flexibility in your vacation days and plans can equal terrific savings on the Internet. If you have the grandchildren for the summer, and you know you want to take a trip but can be flexible with dates and locations, these bargain travel sites are a must-see. The possibilities are limited only by your imagination and by what bargains are available at a given date and time. Due to the extreme discount, there are unique restrictions. Before reserving or confirming anything, make sure you read the site's Frequently Asked Questions to be sure you understand their process. Know that consolidator fares are airline tickets purchased by airline wholesalers and then resold to travel agencies at substantial discounts (up to 70 percent off regular fares).

Be adventurous but consumer cautious—enjoy the extra savings.

www.LastMinuteTravel.com

Every day hotel rooms, airline seats, cruise cabins, rental cars, vacation packages, bed-and-breakfast suites go unsold. LastMinuteTravel.com is a clearinghouse where buyers and sellers can come together and everyone wins. Offers are updated continuously by the companies providing them, and inventory changes. You book directly with the provider. Check back often to this one-stop shopping source for last-minute travelers.

www.11thHourVacations.com

There are unsold airline seats, hotel rooms, and cabins that would like to be sold before it's too late. Look at the same vacation packages others are paying full fare for and purchase at a bargain. At 11thhourvacations.com, you will see available near-term bargains, tours, and cruises leaving in a short period of time, have access to full details of travel times and dates, and make all the necessary booking arrangements at your convenience. Check out their Frequently Asked Questions for more information.

www.CheapTickets.com

Choose from regularly scheduled flights from major airports in the United States, Europe, Asia, and South America. These nonpublished discount airfares on over thirty-five airlines are available through Cheap Tickets. To help round out your plans, CheapTickets.com will also provide great deals on rental cars, hotel accommodations, and cruises.

www.Air-Deal.com

Air-deal.com states that due to the low fares they offer, they cannot confirm your airline until reservations are paid in full, but a major U.S. carrier will provide guaranteed transportation. You type in your destinations and they will get back to you with a fare quote and schedule within twenty-four hours. You may or may not want to be kept this much in the dark unless it is truly an exceptional price. Included on the quote form are questions for lodging accommodations and a car rental.

www.DiscountAirfare.com

DiscountAirfare.com is a full-service travel agency located in St. Louis, Missouri. They specialize in greatly discounted travel within the United States, as well as Europe, Central, and South America. This includes airline tickets, rail passes, group travel, cars, and hotels. Some of their methods for obtaining discounted rates are having student/teacher/youth contracts and being a wholesaler for many of the major airlines.

www.Bargain-Airfares.com

Bargain Airfares is a full-service travel wholesaler, selling air and train tickets, hotels, and car rentals. They are partners with Renaissance Travel under the umbrella of the Renaissance Group Company. They also offer travel packages, such as spring break vacations, ski packages, and full-guided tours for groups.

www.1Travel.com

Think of one-stop travel services and you'll remember 1travel.com. Farebeater is their airfare reservation service. You simply enter your departure and arrival information and Farebeater will perform a comprehensive search of fares offered by airlines, discounted airfare offers, and their own exclusive White Label fares. White Label flights are fares on major U.S. and international airlines where the prices are so low that the airlines have asked 1Travel.com not to reveal the name of their airline and certain flight specifications. Again flexibility is the key to taking advantage of these discounted fares. Full flight details are made available immediately after tickets are purchased.

www.TravelHub.com

Enjoy a centralized Web site where hundreds of travel agents post their specials and discounts. Click on Cheap Airfares to investigate domestic and international flights. Check out the travel agencies' specials. Join the Hub Club for free and have newsletters e-mailed to you with all the latest info on hot deals. Check out Ask an Expert to locate agencies that deal with senior packages and discounts.

www.Priceline.com

Here's a unique site where you can name your price on airfare, hotel room, or rental car. Priceline.com will send it out and see if a major company will accept it. For airline tickets, tell them where and when you want to go, how many tickets you need, what you want to pay for each ticket, and submit a major credit card. Priceline.com will then search for a major airline that will accept your offer and immediately buy them for you. Flexibility is the key to success on this site. Note these restrictions: Airline tickets purchased through Priceline.com cannot be changed, transferred, or canceled. Also, you agree to fly any time between 6 A.M. and 10 P.M. (midnight to midnight for international), making at least one connection.

www.Airlines.com

This site deals not only in airfare and information, but under Reservations you can also set up hotel and car rentals. Click on Save$ to find the latest, hottest deals with major airlines. Register for free to use their services. Airlines.com will take you through a step-by-step guide on how to use their system.

UNCLAIMED BAGGAGE

www.UnclaimedBaggage.com

Ever wondered what happens to the lost luggage left behind at airports, never to hear from their owners again? Here's a Web site that has some of those long-lost items for sale. Look up the different sections and see if you can find a real treasure among them. The items vary from children's books to cameras, sporting goods to clothing. The online prices are reasonable for used items. Quantity and variety of stock changes regularly. Come back often to see what's available.

Unclaimedbaggage.com is based on a store in Scottsboro, Alabama, filled with lost and unclaimed baggage. They also offer tips on the Web site for making a vacation out of visiting the actual store in Alabama. They provide hotel listings and other information.

Cruises

There's a whole world of cruise ship sites on the Internet for you to check out. Many offer 20 to 50 percent off the published rates for sailings, which will make up for some of the added cost of the grandchildren if you take them with you. Cruising can be as exciting and fun for preschoolers to teenagers as it is for their grandparents. To make cruising more enjoyable for the family, major cruise lines now have specific programs for children that include everything from baby-sitting services to computer labs featuring the latest technology for them to use.

Like anything else, you want to shop around to try and find the best deal on a specific ship or cruise destination. Spend a while looking at the different sites to find the best price and package for your next cruise. Compare prices and discounts.

www.MyTravelCo.com

Click on Cruises and you'll find an extensive menu of choices. They have a family cruising guide to check out for available kid-friendly programs offered by each cruise line. Or click on Seniors Over 55 for extensive information regarding the benefits of cruising and answering many questions. Check out Cruise Deals for additional savings.

www.iCruise.com

iCruise.com is one of the Internet's leading sites for cruise vacation travel. Check out their complete cruise ship database assembled online for your convenience, unbeatable exclusives on selected vacations, and a best-price search engine that will help you find the lowest fares available in cyberspace. Check out their Pack and Go specials on the homepage. Under Cruise Categories you can select Mainstream Lines, Luxury Lines, Budget Lines, or River Cruises. Click on The Real Scoop and learn about Heidi Sarna, who writes the Frommer's *Caribbean Cruises* book each year, and her detailed reviews and information.

www.CruiseValue.com

If nothing else, enjoy the music while you browse this user-friendly site. Captain Jeff and Paula Kivet list their weekly cruise specials on the main page. Check out the secret agent prices of cabin closeout deals and read some of the testimonials from people who have used their services.

www.Cruise.com

Cruise.com is owned by Omega World Travel, Inc., one of the ten largest travel agencies in the United States. Check out their Hot Deals. Click on Special Cruises from the homepage to find a menu of choices. Kids Cruises will show you a list of major cruise lines with kid-sized opportunities during travel. Find out which cruise lines offer the most advantages for wheelchair or special needs passengers.

www.Spurof.com

Spur of the Moment Cruises is a smaller site, but it is recommended by Arthur Frommer's Budget Travel Online. Check out Specials and the Red Hot Specials available. Online reservations are not available on this site. You may contact them by e-mail or call their 800 number.

www.CruiseStar.com

There are a variety of ways that you can use this site to help you plan your next cruise. Look for promotions on your favorite cruise line or look under Best Cruise Deals. Check out Cruise Reviews to see how former passengers rate their favorite ship. You can submit your own review to this site. Check out Cruise FAQ (Frequently Asked Questions) for the answers to all of your cruise questions. GalaxSea Cruises and Tours (the travel agency behind the Web site) offers other features to assist your travel plans such as an online luggage store icon and a travel bookstore.

www.Disney.com

The Disney people have their own cruise line that travels from Florida to a Caribbean island with two ships, the *Disney Magic* and the *Disney Wonder*. Click Vacations on their homepage then click on the cruise ship icon.

You will find their schedules and itineraries filled with kid-sized activities, and all your favorite Disney characters will come along for the adventure. Once you've sailed with them, join their Castaway Club for additional benefits and discounts.

www.Cheap-Cruises.com

Cheap Cruises works with all the leading cruise ship lines—Royal Caribbean, Carnival, Cunard, and Holland America. You can use this site in two ways. Click on Travel Navigator for their huge selection of cruise packages, or link to the Web sites of the individual cruise lines for up-to-date information and schedules. When you see a cruise you like, come back to Cheap Cruises for availability, dates, and a low quote.

www.DeltaQueen.com

DeltaQueen.com has three steamboats and a year-round schedule. Take a three- to fourteen-night steamboat vacation on the *Delta Queen* through the heartland of our country on the mighty Mississippi. Or take the *Columbia Queen* and tour the great Pacific Northwest. Try a new kind of vacation and discover the Delta Queen Coastal Voyages: the *Cape May Light* and the *Cape Cod Light* will take you on a cruising adventure. There are nine different vacation options for traveling along the eastern seaboard, in Canada, in the Great Lakes, or along the Florida coast.

www.WindstarCruises.com

Check out the yachtlike ambiance on these 149-passenger, four-masted, computer-controlled sailing ships with deluxe cruise amenities. Itineraries for the *Wind Spirit*, *Wind Song*, and *Wind Surf* include the Mediterranean, Greek Isles, South Pacific, and Caribbean. Check out the Calendar of Sailings for dates and destinations.

www.Windjammer.com

Dress down comfort and nature's entertainment await you as you sail mast ships mostly through the Caribbean and New England. Passengers can relax in the sun or take a turn at the helm or hoist a sail. Enjoy air-conditioned cabins with modern amenities. Meals and complimentary drinks are included. Stops at a variety of ports of call allow you time off the ship for touring and more.

National and State Parks

Are you the type that believes roughing it is a hotel with laundry service and an attached restaurant, or do you truly enjoy overnight stays in the great outdoors in an RV or a tent? Whichever you choose, the Internet will let you see which national or state park areas provide camping or have more modern lodging, if there are fees involved, and whether reservations are needed. (More detail on camping Web sites below.)

Think of national monuments close to home or across the country you can explore over the Internet with your grandchildren. Bring up sites on wondrous areas and check out information to help you plan an excursion for the future. From national forests to high deserts, you'll find a wealth of information and photos to delight and educate.

www.nps.gov

Enter an Internet world of our country's parkland from the National Park Service. Click on Visit Your Parks to search on a specific park, or search by state or alphabetically by park name. This is a tremendous resource of information for checking out natural sights for the grandchildren.

www.US-National-Parks.net

Less formal and more user friendly than www.nps.gov, this site provides a menu of national parks on the homepage. If you don't know the name of the park you're looking for, or if you want a broader search, scroll down and you can click on each state for a list of its parks. Scroll down further and you can click on regions of the country to set up a vacation plan in a particular geographical region. Each national park comes with detailed categories, which answer most questions on a range of topics from lodging and camping to map guides and park details.

www.NationalParks.org

NationalParks.org is a family-friendly site designed to help you explore the national parks and enhance the park experience for all. Click on Meet at the Lodge for areas such as Canteen, which provides message boards for rangers, historians, and people like you to post questions and relay information. Or click on Visitor Center and go into Explore Your National Parks. From a drop-down menu, select places, such as Abraham Lincoln's Birthplace to Zion National Park, from the A-to-Z list of national parks. Each location will provide you with detailed information such as maps and activities.

www.TheCanyon.com

Here you'll find the official park information for the Grand Canyon. You can click on such selections as Canyon by River and Where to Stay. It stands to reason that, with a national park of this size, their Frequently Asked Questions database is enormous. They ask you to type in a keyword or phrase and click on Find Matches.

www.Crater-Lake.com

Everything you ever wanted to know about Crater Lake is on this site. At Frequently Asked Questions, you can find out how the lake was formed and why it is so blue. Click on Lake Information to learn about the history and ecology of the lake. Click on Lodging to find out about the Crater Lake Lodge. Online reservations, however, are not available.

www.ndparks.com

Visit the North Dakota State Parks Web site. Click on Calendar and check out their guide to upcoming special events. Click on the name of each park for a description of the scenic beauty and features such as size of the park and visitor services. There are over a thousand campsites in the state of North Dakota, with twelve of the major parks accepting reservations. The others are on a first come, first served basis.

www.Branson.net

Welcome to an informational Web site on one of the hottest entertainment capitals: Branson, Missouri. You can click on the easy-to-use drop-down menu for instant access to sections on Lodging, Golf, Music Shows, or the Restaurant Guide. By clicking on the bright blue R located to the left of each theater you'll find reviews, written by users, listed for music shows. You can sign up for an e-mail newsletter of Branson area news.

www.TravelWest.net

At the Travel West Network, you'll find a full directory of information for many of the major destinations in the Grand Circle region of southern Utah and northern

Arizona. This includes such places as Zion National Park, Lake Powell, and the Grand Canyon. Select a Location from the homepage and it will take you to a visitor's guide full of details and areas of information. Check out Activities, Bed & Breakfasts, as well as Real Estate for each Southwest natural location.

www.Joshua.Tree.National-Park.com

Have you ever seen a Joshua tree? Come to this Web site to view this unusual specimen of tree. Two deserts, two large ecosystems whose characteristics are determined primarily by elevation, come together at Joshua Tree National Park. The Colorado Desert occupies the eastern half of the park, dominated by the creosote bush. The western half is the higher and wetter Mojave Desert, the special habitat of the Joshua tree. You will find a menu of items from Activities and Calendar to Weather to choose from. Each selection has a gorgeous color photo.

www.gsmnp.com

The natural beauty and the four distinct seasons enjoyed in the Great Smoky Mountains National Park (GSMNP) are unparalleled, making it one of the most visited parks in the nation's park system. GSMNP includes over five hundred thousand acres with eight hundred miles of hiking trails and ten campgrounds. Six entrances into the park include the two main gateways at Gatlinburg, Tennessee, and Cherokee, North Carolina. Gatlinburg and Cherokee are at the northern and southern ends of Newfound Gap Road—the only road that completely traverses the park. In addition, there are more opportunities for lodging at these two points of the park boundary.

www.FriendsoftheSmokies.org

People from Tennessee and surrounding states worked to create Great Smoky Mountains National Park and they are dedicated to raising funds and public awareness of this beautiful area. Check out this great Web site. Scroll down the homepage and listen to a musical rendition of a sleepy hollow in the Smokies or the sounds of an Appalachian sunrise. Click on Events for a calendar of activities. Visit the Online Store for art treasures and gift sets. Purchase an annual membership online and support the Great Smokies. Membership entitles you to their newsletter, a membership card, invitations to special events, and a "Friends" decal.

As I've shown in the last example, you can search out additional Web sites to your favorite parks. You may find supporting groups, additional fun information, and travel possibilities you hadn't thought of or known about are out there on the Net. Go to a search engine and type in Grand Canyon and see how many hundreds or thousands of different Web sites come up.

Camping

As a child, my knowledge of camping was minimal; my mother wouldn't have been caught dead sleeping in a tent. However, I do remember one night snuggling down inside a borrowed sleeping bag in Susie's backyard with a bunch of preadolescents. Does that count? Roughing it in the dark didn't happen when I was a mother either. I have a daughter that enjoys comfort over au naturel.

Along comes grandmotherhood and I've been blessed with all boys. Think I'm going to escape living the outdoors life? Not for long. Web sites like these will help you get the dirt about sleeping on the ground.

www.Camp-a-Roo.com

If you are interested in camping with the grandchildren, this is a site for you. The information here is not for the hard-core enthusiast. Camp-a-Roo.com focuses on easy access to camping, supplies, and short hikes. Let the grandchildren be more involved with setting up the adventures of a camping trip. On this site, they can pick up tips and rules for outdoor safety. Check out the section Family Fun with travel games and games you can play once you're settled in the great outdoors.

www.hcampers.com

Happy Campers is an RV traveler's guide to the American Southwest and northern Mexico. Check out Directory for an easy-to-use map. Click anywhere on the map and find one of over six hundred pages, each covering an area of about sixty by thirty miles. Each page includes an active map displaying the cities and towns, available RV parks, state and national parks, and ski areas. Details of many campgrounds are available with information on size, facilities, and other features, and a legend of icons showing restrooms, showers, or food stores for easy reference.

www.CampnetAmerica.com

This is an excellent camping and RV directory. The homepage shows a list of blocks to click on for plenty of detailed information. The first one is RV Parks and Campgrounds Locator. This gives you a map of the United States and Canada where you click on the area you are interested in for related Web sites.

www.ReserveAmerica.com

Reserve America brings thousands of campsites from coast to coast to your computer. They want to be your one-stop recreation reservation site. Click on Camping, Wilderness, Cabins, or Day Use for your particular adventure. Make online reservations. Click on the map of the U.S. to select a state and explore the campgrounds that can be reserved through ReserveAmerica.com, or scroll down to one of the state links to view a list of campgrounds available for reservation.

www.KOAkampgrounds.com

With hundreds of campgrounds located in the United States, Canada, Mexico, and even Japan, KOA is one of the largest systems of campgrounds worldwide. Check out KOA's camping facilities as some are more than full-service, featuring RV hookups, hot showers and laundry facilities, convenience stores, swimming pools, even access to the Internet. Click on Amenities to see what is available. Click on Directory and browse the list. Detailed information is available for each of their five hundred campgrounds including facilities, activities, and maps. Once you've decided on a site, you can easily make online reservations.

www.GoCampingAmerica.com

Enjoy three different ways to find information on this site. Use the Clickable Map where you can point and click on the state or province of your choice to bring up a list of RV parks and campgrounds in that region. Use the Advanced Search for specific criteria, or check out New Park Brochures for Web brochures about new RV parks and campgrounds added to this site. Check back often as they change monthly. Other features include

Traveler's Tips and Chuckwagon Diner, where you'll find lots to recipes to use on your wilderness adventures.

www.RVAmerica.com

Here is a great place to learn more about the RV industry. If you have questions regarding purchasing one, using one, or anything in between you'll probably find the answer here. RV America Online has a menu of services to choose from, including extensive message boards. Click on Women's RV Forum and find out what other women are talking about regarding RVs or post a question of your own.

www.rvra.org

If you don't own an RV but would like to try one for a weekend or a month's vacation, here's a Web site for you. The Recreation Vehicle Rental Association (RVRA) is a national association of dealers who rent recreational vehicles. Click on What Kind, Type of RV to Rent for short descriptions to help you learn the difference between a motorhome, a mini motorhome, and a travel trailer. The Information about RV Rentals and Travel is detailed and user friendly, and answers many first-time user's questions as to where, when, and how. You can click on Locate a Rental Dealer and click on your state for dealers close to you.

www.SeashoresCampsite.com

Bring your tent, travel trailer, or RV to one of six hundred campsites located on acres of woodland and only
five minutes from Cape May, New Jersey, and Atlantic
beaches. Seashore Campsites features conveniences such
as a heated swimming pool, full hookups, modern bath-
rooms, a camp store, and friendly staff. You can enjoy
daily activities or just relax around a campfire during the
season from April until October.

Camping.net (no www)

This is a directory of camping-related Web sites listed in
an easy-to-use menu. Click on General Information if
you want links to Web sites on everything from RV parks
to camping tips. Separate sections are listed for News,
Organizations, and State Parks.

NATURE SITES

What if there isn't any money for a vacation this year?
Does that mean you can't have fun exploring with your
grandchildren? Hardly. The Internet becomes your vehicle
of choice, a gateway to faraway places, the tram to take
you to fun and excitement, the first and only stop to hours
of enjoyment. The weather doesn't even matter: If it's
raining outside, make it a rainy day travel adventure.

Let the children send postcards to their parents or friends by e-mail. Remember the greeting card sites we talked about earlier? Most of them also have colorful postcards the grandchildren can personalize and send off. "Having a great time" and "wish you were here" still works even at grandmother's house.

www.ENature.com
Check out the wildlife of a particular area, from your own locality to a desert or wetlands region. This is a virtual field guide to thousands of plants and animals.

ButterflyWebsite.com (no www)
Here you can learn more about the fascinating world of butterflies. Tour their photo gallery, learn how to plant a butterfly garden, take a field trip, find a pen pal, and chat with other butterfly lovers. Did you know the expected life of a butterfly can be two to fourteen days? Did you know Arizona has the most butterfly species in the United States? Did you know there are butterfly breeders and an organization called International Butterfly Breeders Association? Click on the Photo Gallery for incredible photos of butterflies, moths, and caterpillars.

www.Birdwatching.com

Birdwatching.com is about wild birds and the sport of birding. It's for everyone who's interested in birdwatching and enjoying nature. You will find some good ideas and products to help you have fun watching birds. Birdwatching includes all kinds of activities. You can explore the world to find birds you've never seen before. Or simply enjoy the migratory birds who come through your yard. Click on Bird Gifts and check out their selection of binoculars, birdbaths, birdfeeders, and more. Click on Bookstore for a selection of informational guides to birds.

www.SmokeyBear.com

"Only you can prevent forest fires." How many generations have heard Smokey Bear's motto? Check out Smokey's Web site regarding our nation's forests and fire prevention. Click on Forest Fun. One of the three choices is Forest Links. Click on it and you'll see a list of Web site links you can investigate, such as U.S. Forestry Service, U.S. Fish and Wildlife Service, and the American Zoo and Aquarium Association.

Making travel arrangements has never been so easy. Use the Internet to explore possibilities, make plans, and secure reservations for trips near and far. Whether you're flying or motoring, there are Web sites and the people behind them to help you.

Cheap and quick traveling through the Internet is guaranteed to help create memorable experiences with the grandchildren. You don't need a boarding pass for these vacations nor do you have to wait in long lines at a drafty airport to reserve a seat. The smile on your grand-children's faces will be just as warm as you sit together and explore at the computer.

All aboard the information superhighway, where the excitement never ends.

The Acorn Never Falls Far from the Tree

I come from a Scottish background on the maternal side of my family tree with the pairing up of two clans, the Bruces and the Baillies. One side, the Bruces, is a very old highland clan—most people have heard of Robert the Bruce, though he's not one of my relatives—and the other side, Baillies, is relatively new in historical documentation appearing in the 1600s. A Baillie is just a new kid on the block as far as most Scots are concerned.

Once a computer and the Internet came into my house, I was naturally inclined to do a search for Scottish clans. I found my wee bit of Scotland at www.tartans.com—The Gathering of the Clans. I found kinspeople of Scottish heritage all over the globe and had an opportunity to communicate with them through message boards. The message boards, divided by clans, were filled with people posting questions about their great-great-grandfathers or grandmothers in hopes of finding someone that could help them learn more about their own family tree.

I posted a quick sketch of my Bruce relatives and waited. I checked back in a few days. A gentleman, who had been successful in finding Bruce family history, had responded. He made suggestions of places to help me in my genealogy research and asked a couple questions of his own. How far back in the Bruce family did my data go? In answer, I posted the earliest names and dates I had been given from my relatives, which went back to a George Bruce born in 1730.

Amazingly our research revealed that my great-great-great-great-great-great-grandfather and his were the same man. Both our records agreed that George Bruce had a son, William, born in 1752. We knew that William Bruce and Annie Ballard married and had a total of six children. I come from the descendant branch of Joshua Bruce; the man on the Internet was related to Joshua's brother, Garland. We were distant cousins! In another three months, we had connected with four more distant Bruce cousins.

What made it more extraordinary was sharing this information with my mother's sisters and their families. It tickled them to learn of cousins across the United States that were part of this enormous family tree. I wished my mom were still here to share in that remarkable discovery.

Genealogy and Family History

Genealogy fascinates grandchildren just as it fascinates ourselves. Seeing the names of their ancestors listed in a family tree and learning where they've come from can be fun. Get some construction paper and glue, and make a tree starting with their names at the base. Let one side of the tree be the maternal side with each branch showing a grandparent or relative—the other side is paternal—and see how many leaves and branches they can create.

Funny, I tend to think of a family tree upside down, not the newborn at the base but the matriarch. My grandmother is the trunk, the solid foundation, on top of a root system of the ancestors. From there the first four branches, thick with the weight of us all, were my mother, her brother, and two sisters. To me it seems the newest babies would start as a bud, just a twig, at the very most top of the tree, until they matured and sprouted leaves and branches of their own.

www.Ancestry.com

A great place to start searching through large databases of personal information is at Ancestry.com. They give you the ability to do a search on a family name through multiple sources such as the Social Security Death Index and more. Most of the information available is free, including the information from Social Security. Ancestry.com will help you go one step further by generating a form letter that can be mailed to the Social Security Department for a copy of your relative's original application for their card. This application would show their mother and father. Social Security does charge a fee for this process. Ancestry.com also has free message boards, divided by surname, where you can post notices or requests for specific names and dates of your ancestors. Check back periodically for answers to your questions or to verify information. You can register and set up a seven-generation, online family tree that other family members can access, or create your own family Web page. (More on family Web pages will follow later in this chapter.) For a subscription fee, Ancestry.com will give you access to more detailed and varied databases, such as Census Bureau records and military records, to further your research without leaving the comfort of your chair.

www.Genealogy.com

Genealogy.com's goal is to expand the genealogy market by reaching millions of people like you with an interest in their heritage and giving them the online tools to explore their own history. Click on Learning Center and discover what the world of genealogy is all about, and find everything you need to start documenting your own family story. Check out Classes, which provides helpful, easy-to-follow online training that will increase your skill level in doing genealogical research, no matter how much or how little you need to learn.

www.SurnameWeb.org

This is a good resource to build on your family's information. It's easy to begin. Type in the surname you are researching and click on Search. If a match is found, click on the link and a list of choices come up, such as genealogy Web sites and researchers doing work regarding that name. You can click on the link Search 3 Billion Records for other resources, or check out their other features to help in your quest.

www.AncestralFindings.com

Quite a busy site, AncestralFindings.com hits you with an array of options right on the homepage. You can do a free name search, or wade into some of the features listed. Click on Cemetery Database for an alphabetical listing of cemeteries across the country. Choose a site and type in the name you are researching. Other free searches include birth records, land records, military, census, and death records.

www.GenealogyPages.com

This is a portal or search engine for Web sites relating to any subject regarding genealogy research. The homepage provides a menu of options to browse, such as Adoption, Associations and Societies, Military, and Ethnic Groups. Click on a link and it will open up an easy-to-use listing of related Web sites. Browse and use as many sites as you wish.

DistantCousin.com (no www)

DistantCousin.com is a free resource to help you connect with your distant cousins, both past and present. They have several online databases, including marriages, military rosters, tombstone transcriptions, and ship passenger lists, which you can investigate for free.

www.OneGreatFamily.com

A relatively new site that is building a global database of family names and dates is OneGreatFamily.com. For a registration fee, they give you an account that only you and your family members can use to type in names and dates of your ancestors, which enables you to build an entire family tree showing multiple generations. Onegreatfamily.com uses a software package called Genealogy Browser, allowing you to see unlimited generations at one time. Another feature is Smart Search. Even when you are not on the computer, One Great Family is working to help you find new leads and information by doing regular searches on internal and external databases.

www.FamilyTreeMaker.com

For a fee, this site offers you a chance to join and use the World Family Tree, a growing collection of family trees contributed by genealogists and users like you from around the globe. It currently contains over 100 million names on more than 160,000 family trees. This is a collaborative community, where you can reach others who are researching the same names as you are.

Family Tree Maker, a software package by Broderbund that you can buy to install on your computer, helps you store family historical information. You can type in your cousins and great-great-grandparents and then print out copies of the family chart and share it with others. Or print out a yearly calendar that shows everyone's birth date and anniversary and snail mail it to everyone. There's an even easier way to share the information with those that have computers, and I'll get back to this later in the chapter with the Web site MyFamily.com.

www.JCRogers.com

Meet Jeannie Rogers. She has graciously put together not only an intense package of genealogy presentations for you, but she also includes her own adventures in finding out about her family. Her résumé reads like something out of a Fortune 500 company. She is Webmaster to many. This delightful Southerner has created a Web site with more information than a cotillion of debutantes.

www.Genealogy.org

Genealogy Online has been helping family researchers with a multitude of free services for years—free because the vast majority of the data found here is created by public records. This means that you can also contribute directly to the genealogy community by submitting your family's data. The homepage offers you a list of genealogy Web sites to peruse. Click on Events Database to run a search by last name. Use Create an Account to add your family's history to the database.

www.Tartans.com

The Gathering of the Clans is an excellent source of information for anyone with a Scottish heritage. Click on Genealogy and you have multiple choices. Begin a search by clans or by surnames. Or start with Researching, a quick how-to guide to start researching your family tree. If you are new to the process of hunting your ancestors, this is a good place to learn.

Grandparenting

Who could be better to discuss family trees, where some branches are heavy and others bent, than another grandmother? Visit these sites where you can learn from, and enjoy and communicate with others who understand the flexibility and weight of being a grandmother. You know the saying, "If I'd known how much fun grandchildren were, I'd have skipped having children."

www.iGrandparents.com

Grandparents created this site for grandparents with the technical help and support of grandsons and granddaughters. Register yourself for free and start enjoying the myriad of information available to you. Topics covered at this site are very expansive: from child development to first-time grandparenting, and from tech help to travel. Computers can easily be the instruments that bring generations together, near or far, immediate families or distant relations. Let iGrandparenting.com show you how.

www.GrandsPlace.com

Millions of grandparents have taken on the responsibility (sometimes reluctantly but always with love) of raising their children's children. Here you'll find a safe environment of support, detailed information, articles on the changes in lifestyle, and links to other grandparenting sites. Click on Legal Resources for an index of topics ranging from a State By State Resource Map to Grandparents Rights. Become a member for an annual fee and receive newsletters e-mailed to you regularly for continued support. You are not alone.

www.TodaysGrandparent.com

This online interactive site will spur your emotions and energy. Click on Questions, Questions for expert advice about grandparenting. The experts at Today's Grandparent welcome your queries about grandparenting dilemmas; just fill out the e-mail form on their site. Under Let's Talk, choose a topic from the list of available options such as Relationships, Access Regarding Visiting Rights, or Child Behavior. Feel free to start a new discussion thread or respond to other grandparents' messages using the buttons marked Post and Reply.

www.MyGrandchild.com

For My Grandchild was established as a Web site to provide an easily accessible source of practical and entertaining information as well as lots of wonderful gift ideas, and to help grandparents make a real difference with their grandchild. Each time you visit MyGrandchild.com, you will find articles, ideas, and interesting tidbits written with grandparents in mind.

www.Grandparents-Day.com

Did you know we had our own holiday? The second Sunday of September is Grandparents Day. The holiday has its own Web site, which is maintained by the National Grandparents Day Council, a nonprofit corporation established by descendants of Marian H. McQuade, founder of National Grandparents Day. Check out Activities & Resources, or People & Projects. Do read about the Forget Me Not Program.

www.GrandparentWorld.com

Welcome to an Internet community designed to help grandparents stay connected with their grandchildren. This site offers free e-mail accounts as well as relevant links and information on shopping, travel, health, finance, and grandkid trends. GrandparentWorld.com is easy to use. Articles are grandparent specific, and you can ask questions of The GrandParent Advisor. Check out the Message Board and visit with other Meemaws, Nonnas, and Bubbes.

www.UltimateGrandparent.com

You may beg to differ, but this may be the Ultimate Grandparent. Find out about Sir Henry and his wonderful life in keeping in contact with his grandchildren and great-grandchildren. Read his original stories. Send an e-greeting to someone with one of his gorgeous hand-designed cards. Check out his notebook pages. What a fascinating man! His insights into being the best grandparent you can be are inspiring.

www.GrandparentAgain.com

Over four million grandparents are raising their grandchildren. Here is an easy site to use for information and support when you find yourself back in the role of parenting another generation. Sections are color coded; categories include Easy Living, Communities, Legal, and Medical.

www.GrandparentsEdge.com

GrandparentsEdge.com is a grandparent helper. Sections include time- and money-saving tips, and quizzes that offer insights into grandparenting styles and attitudes. Check out Ages & Stages for age-specific development notices. Grandparents can also get recommendations on products and activities geared toward grandchildren.

www.sonic.net/thom/oor/

Off Our Rockers, or "OOR," is a site for grandparents raising grandchildren. Read the Newsletter or use the Message Board and Chat Room to discuss your concerns and thoughts with other grandmothers in similar situations. Click on Quippersnappers, the little bits our grandchildren say that entertain and delight all of us.

Reunions

How would you like to have long talks with your former school friends and not have to worry about losing ten pounds before a class reunion? You can do this on the Internet. In fact you could be snuggled in your chenille robe in the wee hours of the morning or enjoying a hot cup of tea in the middle of the day while you are reminiscing with people you may not have seen in years or decades.

Don't you just love the Internet? You can be sixteen all over again, sharing amusing stories or events with people from your high school or college. What about remembering the first throes of adulthood with your sorority sisters, all in the comfort of your own home without worrying about putting on makeup or taking out your hair curlers?

I am signed up with quite a few alumni Web sites under Montclair High School, Montclair, California. The mighty Cavaliers, class of (mumbled-under-my-breath). I have lost hours reading the message boards of MHS alumni walking down memory lane. One interesting fact was how many had moved away from the Inland Empire of Southern California. We talked about first dates at Vince's Spaghetti and football games against Upland High School; we reminisced about the infamous years of Ben Baker, bandleader, and the wild and crazy stunts the band members usually pulled.

Nostalgia is something we all have in common. On these sites, you can reconnect with old friends, make new friends, share memories, plan reunions, and show your school spirit. Go out and remember yours.

www.Classmates.com

Classmates.com is one of the largest high school directories on the Net. You can look at your school's listing and add your name for free. Using additional features on this site requires a two-year membership fee. Check the state and city location of your high school, and then click on the year you graduated. A list of names of people that have already registered with Classmates.com will appear. You can click on the years around your graduation as well, to see the upper and lower classmates that may also have registered. Remember someone from a rival high school? You can click on that school too and see if they've discovered Classmates.com.

www.HighSchoolAlumni.com

HighSchoolAlumni.com has listings for over thirty thousand high schools across the country as well as Department of Defense schools around the world. Register online for free. Other features offered are Alumni Watch, where you can sign up to receive e-mail updates when your old friends register, and Alumni Message, which gives you the ability to contact others without ever leaving the site.

www.PlanetAlumni.com

Planet Alumni helps you find others and keep in touch in an online community of current students and alumni of high schools, universities, and Greek organizations. Registration is free and offers resources to make keeping in touch easy and fun. Additional features include member directories, message boards, chat rooms, event calendars, and reunion planners. You can also keep up with campus news, learn about alumni association activities, register and pay for class reunion tickets, and buy official school merchandise if available.

www.Alumni.net

No matter what part of the world your former school friends are in, you can all link up through Alumni.net. This is a worldwide site that includes other countries besides North America for schools and universities. Europe, Africa, South America, Asia, and the Middle East have multiple listings of organizations and schools on this site. Alumni.net is available in different languages as well. Click on the choices right at the top of the homepage. Registration is free.

www.Gradfinder.com

Gradfinder.com includes members from over 72,000 schools in 123 countries. Not only can you register to your high school or college alma mater, but you can locate your elementary and middle-grade schools as well. If you don't see your school listed, be the one to add it to this site. In addition to alumni directories, other features include online photo albums, message boards, and a reunion planning system.

www.SchoolNews.com

Register for free at SchoolNews.com and access all e-mail addresses of your fellow students. Over thirty thousand schools are listed for the United States, and you can post a personal biography and photo at any one of them. Additional features include posting reunion updates, message boards, and automatic e-mail notifications when other grads join your school. Check out their school year timeline and find out trivia facts for the year you graduated. Do you remember what the top songs were on the radio, what was playing at the movies, or what was happening in sports? Click on and find out.

www.TDYAlumni.com

The Digital Yearbook is for high school and college grads. You have a choice regarding membership. A free registration allows you to view lists of registered students by school and year. For a one-time membership fee TDYAlumni.com will allow you to view other registered students' personal pages, create your own personal page (to which you can add up to twelve photos), and update your personal page at your convenience. Additional features include a link for searching for scholarships.

www.Military.com

All services are represented here, and if you click on Community and Services, you'll find Reunions. You can browse by service and see a detailed list of upcoming dates and locations. Click on Missing Buddies to post a request for information on someone. Type in rank, unit number, years served, whatever you can remember, and maybe you'll hear from them or a family member. Military.com is one of the largest online destinations for the military community. They serve, connect, and inform the eighty million Americans in the broader military audience—active duty, retirees, veterans, reservists, National Guard members, defense workers, family members, and enthusiasts.

www.ReunionsWorld.com

High School Reunions Online is a Web site dedicated to keeping friends connected. Its services provide you the opportunity to keep in touch with high school friends and classmates long after graduation and reunions. It offers a comprehensive list of services, resources, and tools for maintaining high school friendships. Additional features now include military reunions and family reunions.

FAMILY REUNIONS

Since you are busy thinking and remembering the family, what about having a family reunion? I might as well ask, "What about having a nervous breakdown," right? Have you ever tried to coordinate relatives from several states to one specific location and keep your sanity? Someone has gone to a lot of trouble on the Internet to make it easier for those dedicated, highly underpaid souls delegated to be the reunion coordinator.

www.Family-Reunion.com

Let Mr. Spiffy, the family reunion doctor, show you more information than you can imagine on setting up and having a family reunion. This site has a section called Reunion Planner with categories of games, activities, the guest list, locations, and themes. Mr. Spiffy has a great sense of humor, which always helps when you are trying to corral a bunch of relatives.

www.ReunionIndex.com

You can post an upcoming family reunion at this Web site to try and catch the eye of long-lost relatives. Family Reunion List, created by Ben Ford, states they currently have fourteen hundred listings for upcoming reunions. You can set up a free Web page for your family with them as well.

www.ReunionsMag.com

Reunions Magazine Online is a wealth of details and practical concepts for throwing and surviving family reunions. Like all magazines, there are department features and columns. Click on the different titles in the latest issue and find out more about the world of reunions.

www.ReunionTips.com

This easy-to-use Web site by Reunion Research provides planning tips and practical information on products and resources for group reunions (family, school, and military). Created by a reunion anthropologist (with no formal training, he says), its straightforward concept is a breath of fresh air. Click on the links from the homepage, or scroll down and click on one of the keyword links already set up for you.

Making a Family Web Site

Making a family calendar and snail mailing it to everyone can be time consuming and costly. Wouldn't it be fun to have a slice of the Internet just for your family? You could post that calendar for free. A family Web site enables you and your family to have quick and easy access to family information, photographs, or calendars anytime you choose, day or night.

There are wonderful possibilities for creating a unique and enriching family Web site. Perhaps you discovered a diary written by hand on yellowed-with-age pages by your great-grandmother. Maybe you found a stack of letters tied with ribbon from a great aunt discussing her fears during the Civil War. These precious gems, found in dusty old trunks or storage chests, can be scanned into a digital file and preserved on the Internet.

It is more important than ever to create and save the stories of our present and our past. The emotions of the times, the strengths of the family, the day-to-day experiences from the scraped knees to the graduations need to be preserved for future generations. Even if you are not fortunate enough to have records and documents from your ancestors, start recording your life in words and photos for the generations to come. No one has experienced the world just as you have.

This, too, is where setting up a personal Web page for family members comes in. You can have your old black-and-white photos scanned into a computer file so they can be put on the Internet along with the stories of your life. Granted this is more of an advanced lesson in computer usage. But once you are comfortable traveling through the sites and information that are available, seriously think about making up your own site.

www.MyFamily.com

MyFamily.com is a terrific place to create a family Web site. Start a monthly or weekly newsletter, and share activities that only you and your family will have the capability to see. MyFamily.com gives you a free opportunity to set up a calendar of family members' birthdays and anniversary dates, an address book, and a place for baby or vacation photos. Photo album images can be captioned and dated. You can even share sounds and video clips with each other. You can also exchange e-mail with each other in a private community setting where only your family members and invited guests are allowed.

One member of the family becomes the administrator and has the responsibilities of initially creating and maintaining the site. A pass code is given to each family or family member so that all parties have access to the site and can contribute information or just scan the news whenever they like. Not everyone may be as excited about adding information (some relatives are just allergic to writing anything down), but most family members love hearing what's happening.

Family members are able to simultaneously collaborate on their family history research through one site. Unlike having a family tree software package on one or a few individual computers, now each family member can add, view, and update their latest family changes to the family tree. If you are currently using a software package such as Family Tree Maker, you can upload your family tree file to this Web site. MyFamily.com will walk you through the steps of saving the file in a GEDCOM (genealogical data communications file) format and will attach it to your family's personal site.

The Shops at MyFamily.com simplifies family gift giving by offering individual wish lists, e-mail reminders, and providing personalized gift-giving recommendations. It doesn't get any easier. Click on Celebrations Shop for gift ideas and selections to make anyone in your family happy. Check out the selection of memory keepers, colorful boxes designed to hold mementos and souvenirs, as an anniversary or birthday present. Or how about a time capsule?

Members can create and access multiple MyFamily.com sites. This means you can create and participate in sites dedicated to different sides of the family. Your adult children may want to branch off and build a site including their in-laws without having to mix the information into your site. A first cousin may have family tree information more relevant to their paternal or maternal side not related to you. MyFamily.com can accommodate them all.

www.ctw.org

Let your younger grandchildren make their own Web page and share it with their friends and family. The Children's Television Workshop, the same people that bring you *Sesame Street*, offers the children the opportunity to create a My Page on their Web site. Go to www.ctw.org and click on Kids. Scroll down the page and you'll see Build Your Own Web Site. It offers five or six sections where the children can choose graphics that tell something about themselves. Once this is done, the process will take you to a page where you can type in the e-mail addresses of other family members and friends. This will send them the Web site address to click on and view.

PHOTO SITES

What about having a family photo album available on the Internet? No more running to the drugstore to have ten expensive copies of a photograph made for relatives across the country—you can post them just once on the Internet for free. Enjoy sharing various poses of your grandchild's first birthday or of his or her first t-ball game. You can put together different albums, one for each grandchild, or one for each year. You have control over who will have access to viewing your albums.

Not sure how to get your memories on the Internet? Many photo-processing places are offering a compact disc at the time of developing your film. This contains a copy of each photograph from the roll of film in a computer file. These files are what you would post to this

Internet site. If you have a scanner, you can create your own photo file and use them for your photo albums.

Don't limit yourself by thinking only of recent photos. What about your baby pictures? Think of creating a photo album of the past. By scanning your older black-and-white photos into a computer file, it will preserve them in a digital format that will last for years. Not only can you preserve them on a Web site, once they are scanned they can be reprinted at anytime on paper stock to make as many hard copies as needed or wanted.

www.PhotoPoint.com

PhotoPoint.com is a free site that will allow you to place your family photos out on the Internet. You can post unlimited photos and create different photo albums. You are given a secret code to access the viewing of your photos. That access code is what you share with those whom you want to view your darling photos.

www.photoworks.com

Another wonderful spot for storing and sharing photographs on the Internet is ememories.com. This Web site was created to fill the gap between accessible online technology (the Internet) and the fundamental human need for sharing photographs and telling stories about them. This new set of technologies is like an electronic combination of a shoebox, tape recorder, journal, or album for our lives. And it's free. Click on Gallery to see wonderful shots others have included for all to enjoy. Click on Store for personalized gifts using your photos.

www.Webshots.com

Webshots.com is a diversified site. The process we are interested in is My Photos. You can register for a free account, which allows you to set up and maintain your own photo albums online. Family and friends worldwide will be able to enjoy the latest photographs you download. Send free e-greetings using your photos.

www.ClubPhoto.com

Though they develop rolls of film as one of their main services, ClubPhoto.com also offers you the option of creating and setting up your own photo albums here. With free membership, you can click on Frequently Asked Questions for step-by-step instructions on how to set up your first album. You can then notify family and friends through e-mail and give them the access code to see your pictures.

www.PhotoLoft.com

This is a free Web site, but you may have to download their software to activate and use the photo album process. Any scanned photo will work at PhotoLoft.com, and they'll walk you through adding it to your photo album. Click on Help for detailed instructions.

Your family tree may be thin and fragile as a young willow, or thick and strong as a two-hundred-year-old oak; the beauty will always be that it is your family. Together our trees make a forest of diversity and incredible beauty.

The Internet is another way to help us see the beauty of the forest and of our own family tree. It connects the generations of the world not only to the future but also to the past. Communication keeps a family tree healthy. From the days of general delivery at the country store to the days of telephones, cell phones, and the Internet, families have continued to find new ways to preserve the heritage, lessons, and lore of their past, while remaining open to the possibilities of the future.

Go online for yourself and for your family—past, present, and future. Treat your grandchildren to the wonders and the adventures waiting for you on the Internet.

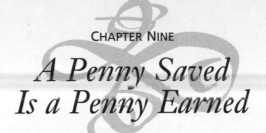

CHAPTER NINE

A Penny Saved
Is a Penny Earned

Do you know the difference between a stock and a mutual fund? Do you know the difference between a bear and a bull market? A bear market is one in which prices of stock are generally declining. Technology stocks went into a bear market toward the end of 2000. A bear investor (and we don't mean just a grumpy Papa) is someone who buys stocks that have dropped in price or when the overall market is down. The bear investor is looking for a bargain while others are being careful. Think of a bear rummaging around in a campground.

In bull markets, prices of stocks and securities are generally rising. A bull investor believes the stock market or the price of a specific security will rise. People are less conservative and buy up large quantities of stock during a bull market. Things are generally going well economically during a bull market.

Whether it's bulls against bears, or the bears are up by a touchdown—it used to be that you could only purchase stocks and bonds through a stockbroker or a profit-sharing program at work. With the Internet comes the ability to purchase, trade, and sell stocks from the comfort of home. Are you looking to begin an investment portfolio for your grandchildren? Do you want to protect your retirement funds? There are many financial institutions on the Web willing to help answer your money questions.

Learning the terminology is important. Don't be intimidated by it; empower yourself by learning the lingo. Look for a glossary on the investment Web site you are using. Use it whenever you come across a term you don't understand.

The old saying "a penny saved is a penny earned," was as true then as it is now. It just takes a lot more pennies. Did you have a savings account when you were in school? Tell your grandchildren there was a time when "banker's hours" meant bankers didn't work on Saturdays, one could only bank during strict daytime hours, and no ATM machines were available.

Teach your grandchildren to look toward their financial future instead of focusing on instant gratification. The Internet is a great place to start a discussion about money. Check out the Web sites for you and for them.

Investing for You

Have you seen the T-shirt that reads "I can't be out of money, I still have checks"? It's not funny if you've seen the price of bounced check charges lately! Whether you are looking at retiring soon or already enjoying the golden years, many of us never stop worrying or thinking about money. We watch the price of food go up, we think about starting a Christmas Club account, and we wonder about saving for a rainy day.

Whatever your circumstances, the Internet has much to offer you in the way of information, support, and customer service in monetary affairs. Find out for yourself.

www.Fool.com

Don't let the court jester logo fool you. That's the whole premise. Two brothers created this Web site with the idea that only the jester or fool could tell the king the truth without losing his head over it. Think of this site as the plain truth. At the same time, they try to throw a little fun into a serious subject. The Motley Fool wants to give you the tools and knowledge to make your own wise and educated choices of investments. Why not enjoy yourself while working with your money? The information and support on this site is excellent. There may be no fool like an old fool, but this site will help you be a secure one.

www.TheStreet.com

Don't think of this as learning the tips and tricks off the street, but rather that you'll be Wall Street–wise when you're through. Start with the section Investment Basics to begin your adventure into the financial world of stocks, bonds, mutual funds, and a crash course on taxes. They'll even break down descriptions of professionals such as accountants, brokers, and fund managers. This is a great place to start learning about investing and with all the other information available, you may decide to stay.

www.Better-Investing.org

The National Association of Investors Corporation (NAIC) is a nonprofit organization that wants to help you invest responsibly for the long haul. Have you ever thought of starting an investment club with a bunch of your friends or coworkers? NAIC has all the information for you to form and operate a local investment group. Think about starting a club in your own family. It does not matter how old you are, you can learn about investing by being part of an investment club. Many family investment clubs contain members that span multiple generations. Ten-year-olds can be nearly as talented at studying stocks as their adult counterparts. You are helping them build a solid foundation of investing that will last a lifetime—not to mention possibly generating a healthy college fund account in the process.

www.Zacks.com

Zacks.com is a carnival of investment information. Their homepage shows financial graphs, tables, and numbers regarding stocks in various industries. Being at the forefront of the Internet information revolution transforming Wall Street, Zacks.com gives individual investors access to research data previously available only to institutional investors. Hundreds of Internet portals and sites such as Yahoo! and *USA Today* use Zacks data to keep their users informed. Click on Portfolios and delve into what Zacks.com can do for you.

www.aaii.org

The American Association of Individual Investors is a not-for-profit organization that wants to help you understand responsible investing. They encourage you to join with an annual fee, yet there is quite a bit of information you can obtain for free. The navigational bar on the left shows Education, Tools, and Community. Under Education, you'll find topics such as Investing Basics. Click here and scroll down to read about starting your investment future from scratch. Check out the other topics. If you feel joining could benefit you, online membership is only a click or two away.

www.msn.com

This giant portal has a reputable financial section. Click on Money from the top menu bar, and you're at Money Central. The navigation bar on the left shows the main areas color coded for your convenience. Click on Investor and you'll have a list of choices to browse, such as Stocks, Funds, and Market. Use Money Central's Research Wizard to find out more about a certain stock or mutual fund. You can find out how a company is and has been doing in the last year. Check out other sections of Money Central such as Family & College, Retirement & Wills, or Taxes.

www.Investorama.com

Here is an easy-to-use starting point from which individual investors can begin to explore the Internet's myriad of financial opportunities available to them. Investorama.com is one of the oldest Web sites; its conception grew out of the realization that people could be reached with information regarding investments by using the power of the Web. Take the Site Tour, and know that your membership to this vast community of investors just like yourself is free. Be sure to take advantage of the message boards and talk with other users who are trying to learn about stocks and mutual funds.

www.InvestorGuide.com

Right on the homepage Investorguide.com offers you a tour of the site to help you use it to its full potential as an investment guide. Learn about how their categories are set up for Business News, Market News, and Stock Quotes. Also learn how to use the toolbars you'll find on each page. It only takes a few minutes and you'll feel more comfortable in how to read the links and sections.

The Investment FAQ (Frequently Asked Questions) is your concise and unbiased guide to investments and personal finance. Find information about stocks, bonds, mutual funds, and options, using their navigation bar on the right. The site even has a Tour for Beginners to help you understand its layout as well as the basic tools of handling your financial future.

Investing for Your Grandchildren

When you look at a newborn grandchild, the dreams of him or her going to Harvard, USC, or Florida State may tickle the back of your mind. When you see the toddler stack his blocks with confidence and creativity, are you looking at a future engineer or architect? When a granddaughter can argue with a ferocious tenacity, is she on her way to a career as a lawyer or judge? Whatever our grandchildren become, we want the world for them. After all, we're grandmothers.

One way we can begin to help our grandchildren's fantasies along is to create a financial foundation for them. The Internet can provide a wealth of information on setting up a savings plan or a mutual fund account, or purchasing bonds for our grandchildren. Investigate the possibilities. You don't have to be a Rockefeller to open an investment portfolio for them. Too many darlings in your heart and family? Then give them the gift of financial knowledge and experience by sharing these Web sites.

With our older grandchildren, we can sit with them at the computer and learn together the intricacies of the stock market. Help them understand the basics now so they can begin to make decisions for the future. You have their heart; encourage them with love to handle their bank accounts wisely.

www.EasyInvesting.com

Learn about Fee Free Easy Stocks and get your grandchildren involved in the financial world. Click on Kids and Investing and read how this site encourages putting the grandchildren's allowance toward kid-friendly companies in a fee-free portfolio such as McDonald's, Wal-Mart, and Compaq, Inc. Click on Fee Free Easy Stocks from the homepage and find out what a "fee free easy stock" is. Check out Fee Free Easy Bonds as well; these are U.S. Treasury Bonds you can purchase direct from the Treasury.

www.Oneshare.com

Imagine buying one share of stock as a birthday or holiday gift for your grandchildren every year. Don't we tend to worry that they get too many toys? Here's a gift that keeps on giving and growing. By the time they are eighteen, with a dividend reinvestment program, they could be holding quite a portfolio when it's time to go to college. Most brokerages do not want to handle the paperwork involved with the purchasing of just one share of stock. OneShare.com provides that unique service online. And you can order the stock framed, delivered right to your grandchild.

www.eHow.com

This easy-to-use portal has an entire section on money. Click on Finance/Business, then click on Investing. If you're a beginner, under Stock Market they have a listing for Getting Started Investing in the Stock Market. Otherwise plunge into the subjects you are most interested in, whether it's in bonds, 401(k)s, or stock trading.

www.SavingforCollege.com

Learn about 529 Plans. A Qualified State Tuition Plan (QSTP) allows for much greater contributions to a child's college fund than an educational IRA. Unlike stocks and bonds, earnings are not taxed until withdrawn. Check out the pros and cons of QSTPs and which are available in your own state. Click on 529 Intelligence and read the Frequently Asked Questions, especially on what's so great about a 529 Plan. Find your state in the drop-down menu and see for yourself if this is an important investment decision for you and your grandchildren.

www.WeidnerInvest.com

Mr. Fritz Weidner has put together a Web site to help you sort through some investing ideas and encourages you to think about ethical investments. Read his article "Grandma Didn't Need a Broker" for a down-to-earth approach about buying stocks. Click on Important Investing Ideas to find a section for Children's Investments and another close to our hearts, Investing before and after Retirement. His approach to DRIPs (dividend reinvestment plans) and saving is easy to comprehend.

www.SavingsBonds.gov

Here is the official site of the United States Savings Bond program. Check out the Savings Bonds for Education section. Learn that Series EE bonds, issued after January 1990, and all Series I bonds are eligible for this program. When using bonds for your grandchild's education, the bonds must be registered in your name and/or your spouse's name. Your grandchild may be listed as a beneficiary but not as a co-owner. Read the Frequently Asked Questions for more details. Additional features include the Savings Bond Calculator to find out what your bonds are worth.

www.PaxFund.com

Pax World Family Fund does not charge a sales fee and you can begin an account for your grandchild with as little as $250. Pax invests in companies that strive to make a better world and improve the quality of life in areas such as health care, technology, and pollution control. There are also other funds available. For information, click on the icons in the left-hand tool bar.

www.eFunds.com

Click on the individual investor icon and find yourself in the Citizens Trust Web site. Founded by Sophia Collier, this site stresses responsible investing and customer service. The slogan "If you wouldn't own a company's product, why would you own the company's stock?" is an example of how much they put their heart in their work. By letting eFund.com put together a portfolio for your grandchildren, you can be sure they've put each company through a rigorous social screening regarding their environment and quality service to the community. Be sure to click on Retirement for advice and support.

www.YoungInvestor.com

Liberty Financial has put together a Web site where your grandchildren and you can learn about investing. The children get to pick a cool name to use while in the site as well as a guide from the eclectic group of characters further down the page. It feels like you're entering a video game, and that's a great way to direct a child's attention to such an important topic. The Kid Comm section asks money questions at children's level. Check out the Parent to Parent section for more information. Additional features include a College Calculator that you can download to your computer.

Before the advent of the information superhighway, I had purchased savings bonds for my grandsons, and now those bonds are tucked away safely for that distant day of their adulthood. Now I'm entering the world of bulls and bears, one baby step at a time. Imagine if your parents had purchased a few shares of stock in a railroad company when you were a baby or a piece of some new company with a funny name like Coca-Cola. I like imagining doing something like that for my grandkids. I'm not looking for the next high-tech superstar. I want something solid and long term that will grow with them. The Internet will make that easy and simple to do.

Online Trading

The term "trading" is the business of buying and selling stocks or commodities—usually through a broker. "Online trading" is the popular action of buying and selling commodities over the Internet. Remember, the

Internet is open all day, every day. You don't have to wait for someone to come into the office to ask a general question about trading. Look on the Web.

As with anything else, shop around before you take the plunge. Find out what fees are involved in making an online trade. What services does an online brokerage provide, and how does using their company benefit you? Most big-name online brokers, for example, offer real-time quotes on stocks. If they want your investment business, they have to earn it, prove they are worthy, or by golly you'll find some other Web site. Do your homework and read the fine print to these Web sites.

www.Gomez.com

Gomez.com is a service site that handles a score-ranking process for more than six thousand companies. Look under Personal Finance and you'll find Brokers (Full Service) and Brokers (Online). These comparison charts and reviews might answer some of your questions or concerns when looking for an investment firm. Click on Brokers (Online) and find out how each brokerage firm was rated. Categories include ease of use, customer satisfaction, on-site resources, and overall costs. Then check the next box on the right for their recommendations if you are a hyperactive trader or a serious investor. This is an excellent resource.

www.Ameritrade.com

You can watch a demonstration of the online trading process by clicking on Trading Demo. This is a great feature for the beginner investor even if you do not use their services. Let Ameritrade.com show you how a transaction is made on their site. Their big selling point is one low fee per equity trade, no matter if it's a few shares of stocks or thousands. Check the fine print to be sure. A minimum amount is required to open an account with their Express Application, which allows you to open an account and trade on the same day. You have access to thousands of mutual funds, and all accounts with Ameritrade are insured by the SIPC, Securities Investor Protection Corporation. Do understand that this insurance does not protect you from stock issues.

www.eTrade.com

As one of the oldest online trading sites, eTrade.com customers can be found worldwide. You can invest in stocks, options, mutual funds, and bonds. eTrade.com can be used as a great tool in understanding investing without actually setting up an account. You can become a member for free and enjoy many benefits without having to spend a single penny. If you decide to become a customer, a minimum amount is required to set up an account. eTrade.com states it does not charge a per-order fee or handling charges; instead it charges a small commission per trade.

www.CharlesSchwab.com

A leader in online trading, Charles Schwab's commitment to customer service is well known. Schwab offers a simple and easy-to-use account application as well as the option of grouping your accounts in predetermined (retirement, grandchildren's education) or customized buckets to help better assess your investment picture. Charles Schwab branch offices also complement this Web site by providing online investing seminars as well as in-person customer service and advice through the firm's Portfolio Consultation program. This is truly a brick and click corporation. They want to take care of you online and from their local offices as well.

www.MLDirect.com

Merrill Lynch's logo is a bull, representing a positive stock market environment. You can open an investment account or a retirement account with the confidence that you are working with a reputable long-standing investment firm. Their financial strength and stability has become synonymous with investing. Existing Merrill Lynch customers can have their accounts brought online to see a comprehensive summary.

www.Fidelity.com

This site has the tools, products, and services that make it a leading competitor in discount brokerage cyberspace.

The Retirement Center helps you not only plan for retirement but also helps with planning once you are in your retirement years. A top company in customer confidence, you will find their quality service covers Web site, telephone service, and their branch offices. Check out their college 529 plans and Uniform Gifts to Minors Act (UGMA) accounts for your grandchildren.

www.AmericanExpress.com

At the homepage, click on Financial Services to enter their online investment and banking process, American Express Brokerage. The same quality company you think of in credit cards and traveler's checks can help you online with your investing. You can set up an individual account, a custodial account for your grandchildren, or a retirement account. Check out their additional feature Roadmap to the Future, an outstanding financial-planning tool that offers suggestions on how you can best allocate your dollars to reach your financial goals.

www.MyDiscountBroker.com

You don't have to pay exhorbitant fees to get quality customer service. My Discount Broker is proof of that. One low fee per transaction instead of a percentage commission is why a discount brokerage makes sense. Check out their quick comparison box at the bottom of the page. No initial deposit or minimum balance is necessary to open a cash account. Click on Learning from the homepage and get involved in their extensive Learning Center. Empower yourself with knowledge.

www.Firstrade.com

At a low transaction fee for market orders and competitive margin rates, Firstrade.com has always been popular with active traders looking to save on commissions and fees. The operative word there is *active*. There is no minimum to open an account. There are no minimum balances or fees for an education IRA, something to look at for the grandchildren. Firstrade.com has features such as research from Standard and Poor's Corporation and Wall Street reports under Quotes & Research. Use their Learning Center and get the feel of the site. And if you need a break from stock quotes, click on Shop @ Firsttrade to go to their online mall for a shopping spree.

Investing is serious business. Do plenty of research, questioning, and checking before you invest with any brokerage company. The Internet provides a tremendous opportunity to educate yourself and prepare your grandchildren for a healthy financial future. If you're already an investor, the Internet has opportunities and resources to help you spend your investing time more efficiently and hopefully more profitably as well.

CHAPTER TEN

For Every Question, There's an Answer

If you have grandchildren out of diapers, you've probably heard the all-encompassing word—why—at the beginning of many of their questions. Why do birds fly? Why is night so dark? Why did the chicken cross the road? Grandchildren are full of questions, and the Internet is full of answers offering you vast resources of information. The Internet can help you answer the little ones' questions, as well as assist you with the older ones' homework. All the while it helps you encourage wonder and support good learning habits with future generations.

Headline news, trivia, reference guides, maps, and encyclopedias are just a few of the incredible conveniences waiting for you. A wide world of wisdom and wackiness is out there on the Web.

News

If you're a news-aholic, you may want to invest in a coffeepot to keep by your computer because there is no end to Web sites on what's happening around the world. You don't have to wait for the five o'clock news for breaking events, or sit back until Sunday morning for *Meet the Press* to get the latest editorials. Just pour yourself a cup of coffee and enjoy the news—it's online, all day, every day. You do not have to subscribe to these news sources to receive the headlines and details of stories and activities everywhere; just open the Web sites. It's that simple.

All the news, all the time Internet-style means you can follow a story anywhere and have up-to-date information as soon as it's available.

www.CNN.com

CNN Interactive is updated twenty-four hours a day, seven days a week, so you'll always have the latest news at your fingertips. Their Web site is organized into several major sections, each with its own main subject page. Using the navigation bar on the left you can click on World, U.S., or Local, which is based on CNN's more than three hundred television affiliates throughout the United States and Canada. News story links are in blue text and underlined; click to see the full story. If you see a small video camera icon next to it, a short video clip is available to watch with that news item. Watch for photo galleries of major stories.

www.MSNBC.com

As the only news organization covering three different media technologies—local broadcast station on television, cable television programming, and the Internet—MSNBC brings you up-to-the-minute news from around the world. Subjects are listed to the left for your convenience. Click on News to find an index of categories and titles of the articles. Top Stories is followed by Politics, International, and U.S. News. Keep

scrolling for further categories, or go back to the homepage and select from Business or Health. If you click
Local, it will bring up a map of the United States for you
to choose the state and then the area closest to your
request. Keep an eye on relatives' and friends' regions
with this feature.

www.CBSnews.com

This multilevel site of CBS TV, Inc., gives you a variety
of options. Use the navigation bar on the left and choose
among National, World, WeatherWatch, and Eye on
Politics. Scroll down a little further on the homepage and
you find easy-to-click links to CBS Entertainment, or
browse the categories on the right for the same links to
CBS SportsLine, or CBS HealthWatch. Easy-to-use
links to top headlines for each section can be found on
the homepage.

ABCnews.go.com (no www)

Do you want just a quick overview of today's headlines?
Either scroll down toward the bottom of the homepage
or click on News Summary from the menu on the left.
Are you looking for a specific storyline? You can type in
a keyword or two in the Search box. Get local news,
weather, and sports by clicking on Local and following
with the link to your ABC-affiliate area. Other features
include easy-to-use e-mail links to your favorite shows—

such as *Good Morning America* or *20/20*—and departments from the Web site. They want to hear your opinion and your concerns.

news.NPR.org (no www)

National Public Radio is headquartered in Washington, D.C., with more than thirty bureaus and offices around the world supporting the quality of their broadcasts. National Public Radio is online and available. Scan the headlines or click on a category from the index on the left. There is also a drop-down program menu at the top of their homepage. Once you've finished with the News, you can highlight your favorite NPR program for the latest in what's happening at *Car Talk* or *Wait, Wait, Don't Tell Me.*

www.KTLA.com

KTLA is the local Channel 5 in the Los Angeles, California, area. Back in 1949 with their live, extended coverage of a child lost down a well, they pioneered the techniques of live, on-the-spot news coverage. KTLA was also the first station to telecast live from a helicopter and the first to use a mobile news van. This award-winning news service is now online for your convenience. Click on News from the homepage and stay up to date with the *KTLA Morning News*, a five-day weather forecast for Southern California, and stories from the *Los Angeles Times*.

www.King5.com

Western Washington's news station is available online. Get a five-day weather forecast with a Doppler radar shot of the Puget Sound area. Use the handy index guide to the left for one-click entry into News, Weather, Traffic, or Sports. Click on Traffic/Cams and highlight Local Cams for video shots of various areas around western Washington. Be sure to check out Mr. Food and find out what's cooking in the kitchen.

www.EOnline.com

E! Online, a subsidiary of E! Networks, provides up-to-the-minute entertainment news, information, and gossip whether you're looking for articles about your favorite actors or movie and television info. Check out their reviews and games, and shop for entertainment-related merchandise by clicking on Shop. Sign up for their free membership and receive e-mail notices of promotions and headlines. E! Entertainment Television is currently available to most cable and direct-satellite subscribers in the United States.

www.TotalNews.com

Total News is a portal or mini search engine to the major news Web sites. When you type a keyword in the Search box, you'll receive a listing of articles and reports from all over the news industry, not just one or two resources. If you wanted to review the Elian Gonzales episode, you could type in the name Elian and scroll through an index of stories from *ABC News* to the *Washington Post*. Want to find out what's happening in other countries? Click on World News and choose from an index of global areas. Then scroll down the list of news sites available for information and stories.

Newspapers

Did your adult children just take a new job halfway across the country? You can keep track of their new location through the online newspapers you'll find on the Internet. Do your retirement plans have you traveling from region to region? You can find out the headlines of where you're going or where you've been by reading the local newspaper reports from your computer.

Imagine having subscriptions to a dozen newspapers to read any time you want. From national conglomerates to local dailies, you'll find just about every area covered, with new sites coming online all the time for free.

www.NYTimes.com

The New York Times is on the Web. Find daily, national, and local news coverage from one of the Big Apple's newspapers. Check out breaking news, updates, technology, sports, and reviews. Under Features find the famous *New*

York Times daily crossword puzzle with solutions printed the next day. There's even a section for Cartoons, albeit limited to editorial artists, plus *Doonesbury* and *Dilbert*. Classified ad listings can be found under Services.

www.LATimes.com

The Los Angeles Times publishes four daily regional editions: Los Angeles Metropolitan, Orange County, Valley, and Ventura County, as well as a national edition you can browse online. No matter where you are, you can take the newspaper with you if you have a computer to use. Keep an eye on the local sport teams from the Clippers to USC. Daily feature sections include Front Page, the A Section, Metro, Business, and Sports as well as editorials. You'll find weekly and Sunday sections available. Discussion boards and crossword puzzles are available with free membership.

www.Herald.com

This site features local news and information from the Internet edition of the *Miami Herald*. Use the easy menu on the left. Click on News and it opens a separate list for regional, state, national, and world stories. Sign up for free membership and have *Miami Herald* e-mail dispatches to your inbox.

www.DallasNews.com

The *Dallas Morning News* is online to serve you with the Dallas Metro news, sports, and entertainment. You can do a search with their online archives going back to 1984 for stories of interest. News and sports sites are updated daily. Their side menu is in alphabetical order, which can be a little distracting, starting with Arts/Entertainment. National/World is further down. Scroll the homepage for columnists and additional feature items.

www.USAToday.com

How fresh is the news at *USA Today?* You will find a date and time at the top of all new stories. That date/time is when the story appeared on the World Wide Web. (Note: The times published are Eastern Time Zone.) Use the index on the left or do a search by keyword. Be aware of "spoiler alerts"—you may not want, for example, to know the outcome of an award show from New York if you live in Los Angeles and the show hasn't been broadcast there yet.

www.Newspapers.com

Newspapers.com is a service for people to use to find newspaper publications from all around the world. They have tried to add as many links as possible. Do a search by state or by country. Check out the menu options for College & University Publications and Specialty Publications.

Graphics are kept to a minimum on this site, to provide easy access to anyone, anywhere.

www.ThePaperBoy.com

Do you know how many newspapers in California this site links to? One hundred ninety-five as of this writing. New York comes in second with 117 newspaper links. Sponsored by About.com, this easy-to-use site lets you use drop-down menus to find newspapers by country or by state. If your grandchildren live out of state, you should be able to stay on top of what is happening in their area quite easily.

www.AP.org

In 1998, the Associated Press (AP) marked the 150th anniversary of its founding. The Associated Press is one of the main sources of news to be published in newspapers or carried by TV or radio stations. The Associated Press is a nonprofit group, owned by its 1,550 U.S. daily-newspaper members. The members elect a board of directors that govern the organization. In the United States alone, AP serves over 1,500 newspapers and 5,000 radio and television stations. Add to that the newspaper, radio, and television subscribers in over a hundred countries, and you'll have some idea of AP's global reach with news. Click on "The Wire" for the latest news in any region.

E. W. Scripps founded the United Press Association in 1907 to cover news from around the world. In 1958, when United Press merged with William Randolph Hearst's International News Service, the name changed to United Press International (UPI). This site does not carry headlines and stories, but has a unique archive of newspaper photos you can search through by clicking on UPI Newspictures.

LOCAL, STATE, AND FEDERAL GOVERNMENT SITES

Learning more about our government will help make a better world for our grandchildren. Learn how to use the tools on the Internet to find information regarding government. Share the information with your adult children and grandchildren. Help to instill patriotism in this instant-gratification, video generation. Use the Internet to build pride in our nation, our flag, and our government.

Maybe you can't fight city hall, but you can send them e-mail regularly letting the officials know what you think of their actions or inaction in your town. You have access to state officials and the president as well. Let your voice be heard, and teach the grandchildren to fight for what's right.

www.First.gov

Make First.gov your first stop for finding information regarding local, state, and U.S. agencies' Web sites. This easy-to-use portal is designed to give you a centralized place to search for answers regarding any form of government. If you don't know what department you need, do a search with First.gov by typing a few keywords into the Search box; it will point you in the right direction. Check out the rest of Featured Subjects area for new Web sites and important information.

www.WhiteHouse.gov

Welcome to the White House online. Former President Clinton and his staff set up this Web site in 1994. You can e-mail the president or the vice president anytime you want, on as many subjects as you want. Sit down with your grandchildren and click on For Kids. Click on The History to find out who's moved in and out of our nation's capital. Click on White House Tours for information on schedules, tickets, and tours.

www.WA.gov

Here is the official State of Washington Web site, Access Washington. Think of it as a portal to the services of state government. Click on any of the subjects listed on the left navigation bar, or scroll down toward the bottom of the page to use the Search box. Most of your questions may fall under Public Services, from Environment and Natural Resources to Health Care and Social Services. Click on Business for licensing information and how to start your own small business in Washington.

Check the Internet for your own state, or maybe your grandchildren's state. Type in the URL address www.WA.gov and before you click okay, replace WA with the two-character reference of your state, i.e., KY for Kentucky, HI for Hawaii. See what interesting sections and services you find.

www.CA.gov

Visit the State of California official homepage. The navigation bar on the left is in alphabetical order with sections including Agriculture and Veterans. Not sure which department you need? Type in a few keywords in the Search box toward the bottom of the homepage and click Go. You will receive articles and information from any data that matches your request. As an example, typing in "dog licenses" brings up detailed information from different California counties concerning licensing, animal control, and local ordinances.

www.FreeAdvice.com

This is a great site for legal advice and law information. The menu of categories is alphabetical with many sub-headings, from Accident Law to Small Claims. Hundreds of topics are included. Additional features include Find a Lawyer and Message Boards. Click on Legal Forms and find legitimate forms you can order and use that have been prepared by lawyers. Click on Wills for All States and choose yours for regional information; you'll see a variety of choices based on your own circumstances—for example, married with adult children, divorced with minor children, or single with minor children.

www.DumbLaws.com

Welcome to Dumb Laws, the Web site to remind you of how far we've come and how far we still have to go with regard to law and order. The information on these sites is true, taken from newspapers and articles over the years. Click on the United States or use the drop-down menu to the left and find your state to begin an adventure into the incredible. Most of these are forgotten laws that are hopefully no longer enforced but are still on the law books. Information on other countries is also available as we are not the only ones with the knack of passing dumb laws.

www.Lawoffice.com

All legal information on Lawoffice.com is provided to you without charge. That's right, it's free. You'll find a database of over four hundred topics to browse. You can select a main category from their drop-down menu. Find advice in areas from adoption to taxes. A searchable directory of more than one million lawyers and legal professionals is available under Find a Lawyer with informational tips on how to find and interview a potential attorney

Magazines

Standing in line at the grocery store, don't you wish you could pick up one of every magazine you see? All those cover pages with their teasing headlines about interviews with famous people and recipes are tantalizing. Especially around the holidays when you're looking for decorating ideas, the Internet can turn into your favorite magazine rack with just a few clicks.

www.LadiesHomeJournal.com

Ladies Home Journal (LHJ) online, can you believe it? Click on Celeb on the Web for feature interviews with your favorite personalities. Browse through the archive of stories as well as interviews with highlighted celebrities. The well-known section "Can This Marriage Be Saved?" is also available. You can click on Her Turn, His Turn, and the Counselor's Turn. Then click on the Discussion Group to join in with your own thoughts or experiences on topics such as family, relationships, and friends. Sign up for LHJ's daily recipe e-mail.

www.WomenTodayMagazine.com

Women Today is a positive, uplifting online magazine for busy women worldwide. Sections include Advice, Beauty, Family, and Career. It offers a nice feature at the end of each article: You'll find a link there so you can e-mail a copy to a friend if you want. Scroll down the homepage and you can read life stories from women in many different countries. Click on Russia, Egypt, Canada, or Yugoslavia to hear another woman's perspective and story.

www.SoapDigest.com

Soap Opera Digest magazine is online to bring you the latest and greatest on your favorite soap. No matter which station you watch, this site covers all the soaps in prime time as well as the much-loved daytime episodes. Click on Features and Interviews to read in-depth stories about the actors and actresses you see every day. Check out VCR Alerts for a calendar of exciting episodes per show. Special Events & Promotions will advise you on public appearances of your favorite actors. If you miss a show, check back here and find out what happened.

www.craftideas.com

Here is a conglomerate of four craft magazines online for your convenience. *Crafts N Things* brings a wide variety of general craft projects; *Pack-O-Fun* is a family craft publication; *Painting* offers painting tips and techniques; and *The Cross Stitcher* carries over twenty-five patterns per issue. You can do a search by the type of craft you are interested in, a holiday or theme that the craft is for, or the magazine where the project came from. Type in a keyword or two in the Search box and click Go. Or check out Tip of the Day. Scroll down to see Today's Features.

www.CraftworksMag.com

Some of the menu items across the top pertain to their printed magazine in hopes you'll purchase a subscription. However, click on Free Project for a new craft idea each month; it comes with a list of materials and instructions. Click on Kid's Corner, where the projects have been submitted by the young generation; it also includes supplies needed and instructions. Enjoy their Message Board. Be sure to check out Sites to See, where there are other Web sites relating to crafts indexed for you by subject.

www.BHG.com

Better Homes and Gardens has an easy-to-use site with all the quality you've come to know in their printed magazine. Across the top, you have menus for House & Home, Food, Garden, Crafts, or Family. Click to enter. You'll see a variety of areas on your screen; each section comes with a discussion group and helpful tools as well as articles. Or scroll down the homepage and browse through the titles of featured articles under the heading Highlights. Click on the blue links to see the story.

www.FamilyCircle.com

This is a snippet of the printed magazine to whet your appetite in hopes you'll subscribe. Scrolling down the homepage will list one article per main heading—such as one recipe, one article on health, one article on money. Click on the Family Circle Travel icon for detailed information regarding vacation plans.

www.MarthaStewart.com

Sign up for your free membership and be entered into Martha's monthly sweepstakes. Receive e-mails regarding highlighted articles and promotions. Browse through the sections of Cooking, Gardening, Crafts, Home, and Holidays. Click on Cooking and you'll see the Kitchen Tip of the Week, menus, and featured articles. Want a glimpse into Martha's calendared to-do list? Scroll down to the bottom of the homepage and click on the tiny print that says About MSO (Martha Stewart Online). Click on About Martha. Scroll down and click on Martha's Calendar. While you're at About MSO, check out her Scrapbook and Questions sections.

www.Reminisce.com

North America's favorite nostalgia magazine has a Web site. Unfortunately, they won't let you read any of the articles in the current newsstand issue of this great magazine. They just wet your whistle on the titles such as "Fill 'Er Up! Remember when attendants filled the tank and gave you a gift?" or "Hats Off, Kid! This 3-year-old started a hat fashion fad back in the '50s." You can subscribe online to have this magazine delivered to your home address.

www.Salon.com

This award-winning online magazine has been featured on *Good Morning America* and written up in the *Los Angeles Times* and *Newsweek*, as well as other leading media. You'll find a variety of topics to choose from such as News, Politics, Technology & Business, Arts & Entertainment, Books, Life, and People. These areas are updated frequently. Check out Salon.com's online discussion area, Table Talk. A sample from the list of topics you'll find there includes Books, House and Garden, Movies, Sports, Television, and Writing.

www.cbhi.org

The Children's Better Health Institute is the central Web site for many children's magazines, and they are hoping you will subscribe once to see some of the information.

Click on the drop-down menu for such delights as *Jack and Jill*, *Humpty Dumpty*, or *Turtle*. These magazines not only entertain, but they teach our grandchildren too. How many of you had subscriptions for your own children as they grew up? Stressing healthy bodies and good character, these magazines also touch on entertaining education. The actual information online, however, is limited.

www.WeeklyReader.com

The best known of Weekly Reader's publications is probably *My Weekly Reader*, a newspaper publication for children in the elementary school grades. Eleanor Johnson, then director of elementary schools in York, Pennsylvania, and a well-known reading expert, founded this famous newspaper in 1928. The first edition of *My Weekly Reader* was for the fourth grade and came out in September of 1928. Other editions were added later until, by 1959, there were papers for kindergarten through grade six. You can spend quite a bit of time browsing through the different age levels and sections of this site. Find cooking recipes and tips, featured articles, and games. Sit with your grandchildren and play some of the activities.

Many of these online magazines have information for submitting manuscripts to them. If in your heart you long to be a writer, look in the fine print at the bottom of the sites for the Site Map. You will usually find the details for submission in the Frequently Asked Questions or around the editorial information.

Dictionaries and Encyclopedias

Back in the late 1950s, it was an exciting day in my neighborhood when a complete set of the *World Book Encyclopedia* was delivered to my house. I was the first and only kid on the street to have such a luxury. I remember breaking the seal of the newly printed pages that stuck together. Each book held adventure and knowledge. It wasn't long, however, before the glamour wore off: Because we had the encyclopedia, my parents now expected me to get perfect grades.

Learning can be a delight, though—no matter how much we groused in those years of schooling. We can keep on learning no matter what our age. Now if we have a question about something, we can just sit down and log onto the Internet, and look up the answer. It doesn't take long and you'll be surprised at what you'll discover, especially if the grandchildren are with you. Make it a family practice to log on and look it up.

www.Britannica.com

Britannica.com not only includes the complete *Encyclopædia Britannica*, but also offers additional features such as a searchable guide to the Web's best sites, articles from top magazines, news, weather, and sports. When you type in a keyword or words in the Search box, your response may include a little of everything. As an example, if you type in Guide Dogs and hit Search, you will see a list of Web sites related to guide dogs, information from the *Encyclopædia Britannica*, and pertinent magazine articles including ones describing the crossbreeding of golden retrievers and yellow Labrador retrievers to make a stronger service dog.

www.Encyclopedia.com

This site is a free encyclopedic reference service made up of more than fourteen thousand articles from the *Concise Columbia Electronic Encyclopedia*, third edition. When you do a search by keywords, in addition to the short detailed explanations from the encyclopedia, you can scroll the page and find Additional Premium Resources, related Web-site links to newspaper articles, magazines, and maps.

Encarta.msn.com (no www)

Brought to you by the people of Microsoft, you have access to an online limited version of the *Encarta Encyclopedia* products that you can purchase on CD. However, take advantage of the Encarta Enquire process at the top of the page where you can type in a question and see the results broken into the encyclopedia resources and related Web sites to click on; scroll down further for additional information provided by MSN's search engine.

www.InfoPlease.com

Information Please is one of the Internet's largest free reference sites. Here you can find facts on thousands of subjects including sports, entertainment, technology, business, education, and health. Type your keywords into the Search box and it will give you a list of reference titles, indicating whether they are from an article or an encyclopedia. Take advantage of the online almanac, dictionary, and atlas features. On the homepage you also have Homework Center and a Biographies search.

www.Dictionary.com

Here you will find—for free—an online English dictionary, thesaurus, and reference guide. Need a definition? Type in the word and click Okay. A list of results will come up on your screen. Trying to find how to spell a word? Type it in as close as you think it may be spelled, and Dictionary.com will show you a list of suggested words. *Roget's Thesaurus* is also easy to use from this site. Enjoy additional fun features such as crossword puzzles and other word games, an online translator for text, and Word of the Day.

www.OneLook.com

This is a great place to look up a word or term. This site has over six hundred dictionaries indexed for your use. This free search access to a frequently updated database of words, terms, names, and acronyms is invaluable. One of the paradoxes of using a dictionary is the fact you may not know how to spell the word, so how can you look it up? Read the fine print under the search box and you'll find you can use the * (asterisk) key as a substitute for many letters and the ? (question mark) key as substitute for one letter. For example, typing in "flo*" would give you any word that started with f-l-o and anything after it (could be thousands of words.) Type in "flo??" and you would get any five-letter word that started with f-l-o.

www.M-W.com

Merriam-Webster celebrated its 150th anniversary by bringing the high-quality references you've known and trusted to the Internet. Back in the 1820s, Noah Webster was on the cutting edge of American English compiling his resource, *An American Dictionary of the English Language*. In 1997, Merriam-Webster carried that legacy forward into the electronic age of technology by bringing their service online. Type in your word or phrase in the dictionary or thesaurus search box. Click on Look It Up.

www.DidYouKnow.com

Fun facts and trivia abound on this site. Click on What Happened, What Year for trivia such as the chocolate chip cookie was invented in 1933 and the LP record in 1948. Did you know that in 1962 Khrushchev removed nuclear missiles from Cuba, but only after Kennedy agreed to remove U.S. missiles from Turkey? Click on the bright red Search button and a box will appear to type in your keywords or phrase. Or click into any one of their main categories for music, animals, sports, and "what's new in the world." Your grandchildren will enjoy the Kids Only section where the information comes in kid-friendly descriptions.

ONLINE CLASSES AND EDUCATION SITES

How would you like to take a class right in the comfort of home from your computer? Enjoy the satisfaction of completing a study course, making contact with an instructor for questions and reference, or chatting with other students worldwide. It can happen.

www.teachweb.net

This user-friendly site is geared for teachers of kindergarten through twelfth grade, yet anyone can use the wonderful resources. Click on Classes for computer lessons and how to use the Internet. You and your grandchildren can go through these classes together.

www.NewHorizons.com

New Horizons Computer Training Centers have been in the computer software training business for years. Now with their Web-based classes you can purchase a session and work at your own pace in the comfort of your own home. Classes include specific computer training certification, desktop publishing, and Web site programming. These courses will give you real-world experience. Easy-to-use exercises and quizzes will help you complete the course. You're given a student log in and password, so you can attend your class whenever it's convenient for you. You can also purchase courses on CD discs that you use with your computer on your own time.

www.WannaLearn.com

Here you'll find a portal of free, family-safe online tutorials and instructional Web sites. Want to learn a foreign language? Click on World Languages under Academic Subjects. You can choose from Albanian to Vietnamese. They list eleven different sites for French alone. Computers & the Internet show categories for e-mail, netiquette, and Internet guides. Check out Personal Enrichment for categories such as improving your memory and speed-reading courses.

www.ed2go.com

A new section of ed2go.com's courses starts on the second Wednesday of each month and runs for six weeks. Click on the list of colleges for the one nearest you. Registration and fees are handled with the college. Each course comes complete with an online classroom where you can obtain your lessons, tutorials, demonstrations, reference materials, quizzes, and assignments right on your computer. Internet courses have classes such as learn how to navigate the Internet or create a Web page. Personal enrichment courses are how to prepare for an upcoming test, eliminate debt, write a successful grant proposal, become a professional writer, or chart a new career path. Legal and small business courses are also available.

To find more courses you can take online, go to your favorite search engine and type "online classes" to see what's available. You may have hundreds of choices to scroll through. Try a different search engine and check out an online class search there as well.

All the news, all the time is right there on the information superhighway. The critics, the columnists, the headlines, and the Hollywood gossip are available anytime you want to sit down and log on. Use your e-mail to share important blurbs and facts with your family and friends. It's faster and cheaper than clipping an article out of a printed newspaper or magazine and mailing it through snail mail. You can send an e-mailed copy to all your adult children and it still won't cost anything.

Don't let anyone tell you that you can't teach an old dog new tricks. If you're interested, the Internet is an open door of educational possibilities. A new word a day, tons of trivia, fun facts, and interesting articles can fill your inbox. Crossword puzzles will help keep the gray matter stimulated. Even if we aren't in the fast lane of higher education, it doesn't mean we can't enjoy the scenery from our own matured perspective, right at home on the Internet.

Who Needs Duct Tape?

Do you ever have the urge to fix something around the home—repair a stubborn toilet, fix a leaky faucet that's driving you crazy, or maybe rewire a lamp you love but have put in the attic because of a frayed cord? Maybe you've never done these things because no one ever taught you how, or maybe you never had any interest or need to do them until now. Or perhaps now that you're a grandmother, you have got more time on your hands to learn some new things you've always wanted to know—and you want to be able to pass these practical skills on to your granddaughters and grandsons.

Whatever your situation, let the Internet give you the terminology, the skills, and the confidence you need to tackle those home fix-it projects. You don't even have to do the work yourself. Just let the Internet teach you a few basics so that when you hire someone to do the work, you will be able to explain what you need to have done in words the repairperson will understand. And later, when the repairperson explains the completed work and what they've done, you'll be able to understand that too. You'll feel great about yourself—and be a better consumer as well.

Home Repair

www.HomeCentral.com

From the homepage, you can click on Home Improvement Guides for a list of main areas. All the help you need for plumbing, electrical work, home and yard improvements, and repairs are right here. Check out Essentials, where you can find tips on picking a contractor and recognizing the warning signs of fraud. Click on Tools and References for additional features, such as their Tool Dictionary and Paint Selector. Answer a few questions in the guide regarding the surface you'll be painting and the Selector will come up with a suggestion for the best type of paint.

www.DoItYourself.com

Easy-to-use, drop-down menus are listed across the top of the page. Do you want to build or remodel, or repair or fix it? Do you want to decorate indoors or fix something outdoors? Would some information on Living and Finance be helpful? Check out the sections and with each category find simple step-by-step instructions for most projects. Simply click on the How To icon for a menu of options, from appliance repairs and fix-its to mortgage loan calculators. Scroll down and you'll find a section for free literature on paint, tools, doors, and floors. This site has been recommended by Women Central, a division of MSN (Microsoft).

www.HomeDepot.com

You can even find those helpful people in orange aprons on your computer. What could be better than customer service on the Net? Across the top of the site are easy-to-use home improvement tabs marked Fix It, Build It, Grow It, Decorate It, Install It. Each one will open a page with a drop-drown menu of projects or ideas. Check out Fix It, where you'll get step-by-step guidance to fix and maintain all kinds of things around your house. Fix It categories include Electrical, Doors, Decks, and Walls. With Build It you'll get professional advice and instruction on how to build all kinds of things like shelving and storage space. Check out the Online Store feature. Type in your zip code and place your order online. It can be picked up at the Home Depot nearest you. (This service is not yet available in all areas. Check online to see if it's available in your area.)

www.PaintedHouse.com

Come visit Debbie Travis's *The Painted House* Web site. Her cable television show, packed with great decorating ideas for every type of home and all sizes of budgets, is seen in over fifty countries. Now get her tips and tricks right here on your computer. Click on About Each Show to see the title of the show and what room or area was used as the subject. You can click on the main topics of the show and/or request to purchase a video at Debbie's

Shop. Check out the Frequently Asked Questions for a barrage of answers to painting concerns.

www.FurnitureGuys.com

Joe L'Erario and Ed Feldman are *The Furniture Guys* and/or *Men in Toolbelts* depending on which cable show you've been watching. On Sunday mornings on the Discovery Channel, these two make working with your hands seem like child's play. Though you won't get their actual information on this site, check out their television schedule or live and in-person events calendar. You can also e-mail them with your questions.

www.Easy2diy.com

The name Easy to Do It Yourself starts you off in a positive frame. This is a full-service site for home improvement projects and home repair. You'll find tutorials, resources, and products as you browse through the site. The menu on the homepage is simple and laid out in a variety of categories from Appliances to Windows & Doors. Check out the Frequently Asked Questions.

www.eHow.com

This mega how-to-do-everything site is user friendly and a great resource. Click on Home and Garden. The index lists everything from Building and Remodeling to Home Repairs and Maintenance. Check out Home Repairs and you'll see hundreds of solutions to problems under categories such as Appliances, Electricity, and Carpentry. Each project has easy-to-follow steps, a warning section of possible hazards and things you should know, and an area where other users can leave their own tips related to the project. If you don't want to browse, type in your request in the How To box and click Do It.

www.AllExperts.com

This unusual site gives you a hands-on chance of asking your specific question to a professional expert at no cost. Browse through the categories until you find the area of your concern, say wallpapering. Allexperts.com shows you a list of professional people and their background. Pick one you like and click on the link Ask a Question. You'll find thousands of volunteers, including lawyers, doctors, engineers, and scientists, waiting to answer your questions. All answers are free and most come within a day; they guarantee an e-mail answer to your question within three days.

www.NaturalHandyMan.com

Here's an easy-to-use site for help, humor, and support with home repairs. Click on Articles and you'll find a drop-down menu of topics to choose from. Highlight one and click Go. If basement dampness is a problem at your house or if a drawer's not working, you get answers fast here. You'll read personable information with tips and tricks to help you solve your problem. You can do a search by keywords with the handy Search box. Due to the volume of questions they've received over the years, their Q & A (question and answer) process will ask you to use the Search box.

www.Housenet.com

The main sections of this immense support site include Home Improvement, Home Decorating, Lawn and Garden, Sewing Ideas, Real Estate, and Smart Savings. Each is packed with volumes of free advice, projects, and how-to articles. You'll find instruction on everything from fixing a faucet to major remodeling projects. Use their message boards, staffed by home professionals from all areas of home and garden, as a great way to get answers and exchange ideas. Be sure to check out their other special features including handy project calculators, monthly maintenance task lists, chat sessions, and gardening tips for your areas.

www.Toiletology.com

Here is the toilet repair site for women, created by a woman. After years of presenting her successful and award-winning Plumbing Repair Clinics, Kay Keating now shares her talent and tips online for us. This easy-to-use Lesson Plan for the Care and Repair of Toilets covers such topics as How a Toilet Works, Emergencies—Clogged Toilets, and Testing for Leaks. Be sure to check out the Just for Fun links. This is no ordinary potty humor.

www.HomeDoctor.net

Here's a self-help guide for home repairs and maintenance. Use it as a free exchange tool for questions and answers from neighbor to neighbor. Click on Self Help Tips and find a menu of categories ranging from Blinds and Electrical to Tools and Gadgets. If you don't find a solution, click on Ask the Expert and fill in the e-mail form. If you've had success with a project, post the information here and share it with others.

www.FurnitureWizard.com

The Wizard lives just outside Aspen, Colorado, and offers you a site for the restoration of furniture and antiques, including repair tips. An easy-to-use navigation bar is to the left with categories for Refinishing Techniques and Furniture Repair Strategies. Also check out Home Improvement Tips and Care & Maintenance. In the Open Discussion Forum, you can ask any question about your projects and get answers from other furniture do-it-yourselfers.

www.MisterFixit.com

Here is Brother Bob's Web site for repairs and maintenance. Scroll down the index and check out categories
such as Electronics, Plumbing, Tools, and Household
(general). Each one will take you to a list of his instructions and tips on various problems, from damp base-
ments to hissing toilets. In some areas he will suggest
visiting another Web site for more detailed assistance
and has provided the link to get you there.

Earlier I said my sewing skills were, at best, minimal. (I
fix hems with Scotch tape.) Well, my home repair talents
are at the same pathetic level. I can paint a room and
hang a picture straight—end of talent. Once I owned a
toolbox that had more in it than just empty space. Back
in the 1970s, the days of women's lib, I had my own set
of screwdrivers and pliers, a couple of hammers, and a
wrench. They were Sears Craftsman products, only the
best for my toolbox. Of course, that doesn't mean I used
them very often—though a couple of them made great
spider stompers.

I can take apart a computer and put it back together
with no problem. My black-cased computer tool kit is
worn and well used, with all my tiny tinkering toys for
replacing memory chips and adding a new hard drive.
But hissing toilets? I don't think my Scotch tape trick
would work.

Automobile Information

When I buy a car, I buy one brand-new right off the car lot. Then I drive it for years and years until the poor thing is ready to give up its fuel pump. Ten years and two hundred thousand miles later I think about getting a new car and start all over again. My car becomes one of the family. It goes wherever I go—heck, it takes me wherever I want to go.

I bought a Plymouth Arrow before people in my family had even heard of the car. Remember the commercial, "Me and my Arrow?" Okay, neither did my father. What a great little car it turned out to be. I didn't test-drive it, I didn't even know too much about it other than the commercial, and I liked its looks. Oh, and the price was right. I am a car salesperson's dream. Same thing happened over a decade later when I bought my Celebrity station wagon. I knew what I wanted, and I bought it. Another great car.

On the subject of maintenance, just like your kids, your car doesn't really come with a how-to manual. When it starts acting up and making a clanking sound, the car isn't going to tell you what's wrong with it. Nor does it come with a reference guide that says do this and the clanking sound will go away.

There are Web sites, though, that want to help you help your car. These are just a few of the sites available to you.

www.CarTalk.com

National Public Radio listeners, your favorite car repair aficionados have a Web site. Meet Click and Clack, the Tappet Brothers, or Tom and Ray Magliozzi as their mother named them. Their *Car Talk* radio shows and newspapers columns are the mainstay of this hilarious but extremely talented pair. Click on Our Lousy Radio Show, and scroll down to the link Listen To Car Talk. They have broken up their weekly show into ten segments that you can listen to over your computer speakers. Scroll down to see the subject matter. Click on Back Track for past shows you may have missed.

www.Autoshop-online.com

What if you could ask someone, other than your mechanic if you have one, about what's wrong with your car? What if you could anticipate what major repairs may come up in your car's future? Wouldn't it be great if you could get assistance from factory-trained technicians and do the repairs on your car yourself? This site will help you do all that and other auto-repair projects. Click on Automotive 101 for basic knowledge and instruction of how different systems in a car work. Click on the various icon graphics to read about Air Conditioning and Heat Systems, Exhaust Systems, Cooling Systems, and Braking Systems. Car maintenance tips are provided by newsletters from the Car Care Council.

www.about.com

At this portal of nonstop information, click on Autos, click on Auto Repair, and find a variety of topics to browse. The first choice under Subjects is Do It Yourself. This takes you to a list of helpful how-tos for such processes as changing your oil, disc brakes, or fuel pump, and replacing your battery. Troubleshooting is another good area to check out for diagnosing a car problem.

www.FamilyCar.com

Find tips on selecting your next new or used vehicle, learn how to care for it with preventive maintenance, how to handle minor repair problems, and how to find a good repair shop. These easy-to-click-on subjects are printed across the top of the site. Under Car Repair you are directed to Fred's Garage. Check out the section Does Your Car Do This? for common symptoms and what to do about them. Click on Ask Fred to see what other do-it-yourself mechanics are asking. Driving Tips has some excellent advice, such as being sure that children between four and eight years old use booster seats while riding in a car. Is your grandchild safe in your car?

www.CarParts.com

Here's an online store for things you'll need for your car, truck, or SUV. The easy-to-use menu on the front page is divided into sections such as Replacement, Accessories,

Performance, Tires and Tools, and Shop Supplies. To use these sections, first type in the make and model of your car. You'll see the area right above the index table with a little car icon that reads Change. Click there. Use their online shopping for all your car's needs.

www.ShellStations.com

Click into one of the Shell stations, click on Car Problems?, and then click the Answer Book. Here you'll find information and car tips in five main subjects: Prevention, Emergencies, Driving Skills, Security, and Shopping. Under each of these are the answers you'd find in the printed books passed out at local Shell stations across the country. Quality customer service comes through on their Web site as it does at their stations. Use the Ask Our Mechanic process to e-mail a specific question to their experts. They'll get back to you by return e-mail.

www.WomanMotorist.com

Here's a Web site just for us. It has a little bit of everything having to do with vehicles—new, used or otherwise. Click on Maintenance and you can get answers and information from qualified technicians at FemmeTech. Scroll down the page until you see a list of categories. Click on any one of them to find questions and answers specific to that subject. Click on Chat to go into an online chat room where you can discuss your automotive problems with other do-it-yourself participants.

www.AutoRepair2000.com

Need to find a new auto repair shop? Here's a Web site to help you. It's easy. Across the top of the page, you'll see Auto Body & Paint Shop Finder. Click on this if you're looking for body repair for your car. Next to that is the link Auto Service & Repair Shop Finder. Click here and find your state. Click on it. Then will come a list by counties in your state. Either scroll down or click on the alphabet letter to find your county. Then click on your city for a list of shops and their addresses.

We are grandmothers, hear us roar. With the Internet to guide us, we can do anything. We've always been able to banish monsters from under the bed, make dinner out of nothing, and find a missing shoe with our x-ray vision. Now we have the information to take our talents a step further, into repair and maintenance. We are armed and we are dangerous.

Get the grandchildren to help you. If they are old enough, show them the sites on the Internet, and discuss what they think your repair options are. You'll be amazed at their creativity in solving problems. They are also great at handing you tools or nails, and they will keep you company during a project.

If you're fortunate enough to have a teenaged grandson around, definitely get him involved with you. Give him some insight in working alongside a woman, even if it is his Nonna. You will be doing two good things in one. Your repair project will get done and you'll have advanced his gender education toward that Alan-Alda-caring-male degree.

It's a miraculous event when a baby comes into the family. A phenomenal little bundle of life joins the world, and everything changes. The sun shines brighter during the day, rain sounds like a lullaby from nature, and strangers will stop on the street to talk to you about how cute or how precious the baby is. Adults will become cutesy and find themselves smiling around this tiny being.

Okay, the reaction to being online with the Internet isn't quite the same. But in the last decades of the twentieth century, the World Wide Web became an addition to our lives. It's one that makes the day more interesting, more colorful, and allows us to talk to strangers all over the world about how precious our grandchildren are. What a wonderful contraption.

If you're a grandmother or a fairy grandmother, I want you to enjoy the conveniences of the Internet. Find out how simple it can be to do your holiday shopping. No parking hassles, no long lines in a crowded mall. Just you and a computer linked to the Internet.

Convenience—what a great concept. The washing machine and dryer gave us convenience over a ringer action machine and clothesline. The microwave oven gave us convenience over the stove. The car gave us convenience over the horse and buggy. The Internet is another appliance that adds convenience to our lifestyles.

We're grandmothers, we want more, we've earned it. We want to stay in contact with those darling little grandchildren. Communicate with them, every day or as often as possible. Laugh with them, share stories with them. The Internet can do this for you. E-mail and e-greetings are quick, easy missives to send to the children. You could send them an animated e-greeting of celebration for their first day of kindergarten. Make up a reason, make it Be Kind to Butterflies Day, send an e-greeting.

Don't we want to share the grandchildren's delightful antics with all our friends, relatives, and even complete strangers should they ask? Digital photos can be sent over the Internet to a long list of people with the click of a mouse. The first wobbly steps of a toddler, the first time the little one looks up at you and says, "Peeze, Gamma," are important moments. With free e-mail you can send off a snippet or a novella of this news, as often as you'd like, without breaking the bank or standing in a long line at the post office.

We've covered convenience and communication. What about knowledge? Is the old saying "feed a cold, starve a fever" correct, or is it the other way around? Is the left side of a boat called port or starboard? You cannot beat the Internet for fast, friendly information. This is a library/book store/resource center that's open twenty-four hours a day, every day. Don't argue with your best friend over who played the leading role in the comedy movie *It Happened One Night*. Go on the Internet and find out. Stuck on a crossword puzzle? Okay, I won't encourage cheating, but you could look up possible word suggestions on the Internet.

We're not getting older, we're getting better. Let the Internet open doors for you in learning new skills, speaking a new language, or finding out how to do simple home improvement projects. When we feel good about ourselves, it reflects back onto the grandchildren. They too learn to feel better about themselves by watching us, by emulating our moods and our habits.

Have fun with the Internet. Life's too short not to. I encourage you to go online and stay online for the enjoyment of what the Internet can do for you.

Tell others what they're missing. That's what this book is about. From one grandmother to another, I want you to get the most out of these exciting years.

Grandma ONLINE

canning, 192–195
Car Care Council, 337
card games, 146, 147
    casino, 150, 151
cards. *See* e-greeting cards
career tips, 314
Caribbean Cruises (Frommer), 236
Caribbean vacations, 217, 219
CarParts.com, 338–339
cars. *See* automobiles
CarsDirect.com, 46–47
Carson, Dr. Lillian, 25
CarTalk.com, 337
cartoon character activities, 169
cartooning, 175
CartoonNetwork.com, 167–168
cartoons, 142, 143, 144, 306
    about belly dancing, 209
cartoon stories, 168–169
casino games, 146–147, 149–151
cbhi.org, 317–318
CBS alliance companies, 41, 47
CBS.com, 171
CBSHealthWatch.com, 113
CBSnews.com, 302
CCVideo.com, 58–59
cdc.gov, 115–116
CDNOW.com, 56
CDs, 49, 55–60
    flute music, 185
    used, 59
CelebrateExpress.com, 160
celebrities, news about, 313
cemetery database, 258
Centers for Disease control and
    Prevention (CDC), 115–116
ceramics, 182–183
charities
    donating automobiles to, 48
    volunteering at, 202–207
CharlesSchwab.com, 296

chat rooms, 22–23
    for arts/crafts, 175
    auto problems, 339
    health, 114
    home and garden, 333
    other grandparents, 24
    school alumni, 267
    weight-loss and dieting, 122, 127
    writers, 49–50
    See also message boards
Cheap-Cruises.com, 237
CheapTickets.com, 230
cheese, 72
chefs, 81
child development, 106, 107, 262,
    263, 265
    health and, 116
    teenagers, 110
ChildFun.com, 178
Children's Better Health Institute, 317
Children's Television Workshop, 167
Chocoholic.com, 88
chocolate, 75, 87–88
Christies.com, 36–37
chutney recipes, 196
Citizens Trust, 292
classes on the Internet, 323–326
classified ads. *See* newspapers
Classmates.com, 266–267
class reunions, 265–270
Claus.com, 141
clay imprints of hands/feet, 179
clothing. *See* apparel
clowns, 161
ClubHolidays.com, 219
ClubMed.com, 216–217
ClubPhoto.com, 278
clubs
    book-of-the-month, 50
    CDs, videos, and DVDs, 57
    dieting support, 128–129

clubs *(continued)*
  fan, 59, 60
  Fancy Food Gourmet, 85
  investment, 285
  Pavilions ValuePlus, 94
  stickers and stationery for kids, 28
CNN.com, 301
coastal travel
  along the eastern seaboard, 238
  on Columbia Queen (steamboat), 237
  East coast camping, 248
Coastal-Travel.com, 218
cocoa, 89
coffee, 88, 89
coffee cakes, 90
collectibles, 35, 51–55
  toys, 156
Collectibles.com, 54
CollectiblesToday.com, 52–53
college, saving for, 287, 290
  college calculator, 293
college classmates, 267–269
college newspapers, 307–308
Colorado, 242–243
coloring, 138, 139
ColumbiaHouse.com, 57
Columbia Queen (steamboat), 237
comics, 143, 145
computer ergonomics, 5
computerese, 15–16
computer training classes, 324
Concise Columbia Electronic
  Encyclopedia, 320
consolidator fares, 229
contests for grandma, 65, 145, 146,
  148–149, 149–151, 171, 316
contests for kids, 73, 140, 166, 169
contractors, choosing, 329
cookies, 78–79
cooking
  articles about, 315, 316

dictionaries, 79, 81
for grandma, 76–81
for kids, 67–76
See also recipes
Cooking.com, 79
cooking shows, 81, 304
CookingWithPatty.com, 77
cookware and dinnerware, 78–79, 82,
  194, 195
CoolList.com, 26
costumes, 162
country-western dancing, 211
courses online, 323
cousins, locating distant, 259
craftideas.com, 314–315
Craftopia.com, 180, 190
Craftown.com, 177
crafts
  articles and magazines about,
    314–315, 316
  needlecrafts, 188–191
  projects for kids, 138, 140, 175–178,
    315
  selling, 190
  See also art projects
CraftstoKids.com, 179
CraftworksMag.com, 315
craps (game), 151
Crater-Lake.com, 241
CrayolaKids.com, 138
CreativityPortal.searchking.com, 181
credit card information, 22
Critics Choice Videos, 58–59
crocheting, 207
Crochet.org, 189–190
Cross Sticher (magazine), 315
crossword puzzles, 147, 306, 322
Cruise.com, 235–236
cruises, 234–238
  FAQs and reviews, 236
  packages, 225, 226, 237

Grandma ONLINE

Grandma ONLINE

About The Author

A computer technician for nearly two decades and a former two-term president of the Southern California chapter of Municipal Information Systems Association of California (MISAC), Kathleen Shaputis now focuses on her writing and teaching career. Kathleen teaches a variety of computer-related classes for older adults at

the local YMCA and leads workshops based on *Grandma Online*, which encourage grandmothers and fairy grandmothers to explore the Internet. Kathleen's patience and humor have instilled confidence in even the most computer-phobic user.

Born and raised in Southern California, Kathleen now lives in Olympia, Washington with her husband, Bob. She is the happy grandmother of three grandchildren: Joshua, Isaiah, and Taylor.